# COPING SKILLS FOR TEENS™ WORKBOOK

RELAXATION

MOVEMENT

DISTRACTION

PROCESSING

SENSORY

## 60 Helpful Ways to Deal with Stress, Anxiety and Anger

### Janine Halloran, M.A., LMHC

Author of the #1 bestselling Coping Skills for Kids Workbook™

Coping Skills for Teens Workbook

For information contact:

Coping Skills for Kids/Encourage Play, LLC

288 Grove Street #321

Braintree, MA 02184

http://www.copingskillsforkids.com

Book Editing by Amy Maranville, Kraken Communications

Cover design by Meg Garcia, Mabel & Bean Co.

ISBN: 978-1-7333871-7-0

First Edition: March 2020

10 9 8 7 6 5 4 3 2 1

# Dedication:

This workbook is dedicated to all of my adolescent clients, past and present. You've taught me so much, and I hope you never forget how incredible and awesome you are.

Find more online at copingskillsforkids.com

**Books and products in the collection:**

**Coping Skills for Kids Activity Books™:**

Processing Feelings

My Happiness Journal

Relaxation Round Up

**Coping Skills for Kids Coping Cue Cards™:**

The Discovery Deck

The Relaxation Deck

The Distraction Deck

The Movement Deck

The Sensory Deck

The Processing Deck

and

**Coping Skills for Kids Workbook™**

# TABLE OF CONTENTS

# A NOTE TO PARENTS/GUARDIANS

As a therapist, I've worked extensively with children, teens, and their families. Over the last several years, I've noticed an increase in stress and anxiety in all of my clients. That's what led me to write the Coping Skills for Kids Workbook.

But there's also been an uptick specifically in teen anxiety and stress. As a therapist, I know that the teenage years have always been challenging, both for teens and for the adults caring for them; but a recent study suggests that teens now are more stressed, anxious, and depressed than teens were in the Great Depression. The emphasis on grades, structured after-school activities, and the college process has intensified over the years. Social media has also changed how teens interact with one another - instant contact can be a blessing and a curse.

I wrote this book to help teens combat what they are facing. I want them to know that it's okay to experience lots of different feelings - what matters is what you do to express those feelings. I also want them to understand that life is not, nor will it ever be, Instagram perfect. My goal is to help them figure out some healthy and safe ways to manage their emotions, and encourage them to find at least one person in their life they can talk to about their feelings and experiences.

This book is written to teens so that they can read it on their own. However, you can do a book club with your teen and read it together, or use it as a starting point for conversations around healthy coping strategies.

To make it easier to explore coping skills, the book is divided into coping styles. This makes it a little bit easier to find the type of coping skill your teen needs, depending on the emotions they are feeling, where they are when they are trying to manage their anxiety, stress or anger (at home, at school, etc) and what they prefer. It doesn't have to be read in order; instead, your teen can pick the section or skill that they need.

This book is meant to help teens but it is not a replacement for therapy, nor is it meant to help manage a crisis situation. At the back of the book, I've included some information on who to call when a teen is in crisis in the U.S., Canada, the UK, and Australia. It is not an exhaustive list, but it could be a good place to start if your child needs help immediately.

Also, a teen may benefit from working with an individual therapist to talk and explore their own specific experiences. To make it a little easier, I have some suggestions about how to go about starting to look for a therapist in the back of the book.

Also included in the back of the book are some of my favorite resources (specifically for teens) that I recommend to my adolescent clients regularly. I list helpful apps to track emotions and for relaxation, plus books, card decks, and other online resources for mindfulness, anxiety, stress, and anger.

Being a teenager has never been harder. I hope this book helps to ease some of the stress and pressure that so often accompanies this time in their lives.

# A NOTE TO PROFESSIONALS

Over the last few years, I've spoken around the United States to parents, counselors, educators, and other professionals who work with children and teens about my work in the Coping Skills for Kids Workbook. From day one, the feedback I got was "This is great. Now you need to write one for teens." This book exists now because of that feedback.

I started working with children and teens right after I finished college. The teenage years have always been challenging, both for teens and for the adults caring for them. Teens get stressed about lots of different things. According to the Stressed in America survey done by the American Psychological Association, teens worry about things like doing well in school, getting into college, and family finances.

Over the last several years, I've noticed an increase in stress and anxiety, especially in my teen clients. When I talk with other professionals - counselors, educators, psychologists, etc - they have noticed it, too. A recent study suggests that teens now are more stressed, anxious, and depressed than teens were in the Great Depression. The emphasis on grades, structured after school activities, and the college process has intensified over the years. Social media has also changed how teens interact with one another - instant contact can be a blessing and a curse.

I wrote this book to help teens get a handle on stress, calm their anxiety, and manage their anger. I want them to know that it's okay to experience lots of different feelings - what matters is what you do to express those feelings. My goal is to help them figure out some healthy and safe ways to manage their emotions and handle the imperfections of life.

A question that I get asked frequently is if my work is "evidence-based". According to the American Psychological Association (2006), evidence-based practice means "the integration of the best available research with clinical expertise in the context of patient characteristics, culture, and preferences." I've written this book with this definition in mind. I've included research studies about a variety of coping skills and their effectiveness in the bibliography, and in some of the explanations of the different skills, I've noted that research. In addition, I've included coping skills that I've tried with clients throughout the years that have worked well. Just as important, I've listened to my clients. They share their successful strategies with me, and then I integrate that into my coping skills work.

This book is written to teens so that they can read it on their own, but can also be used in your work with adolescent clients. You can work through the book together, pull worksheets from the book into your clinical work, or use the text as a starting point for conversations around healthy coping strategies.

This book is divided into coping styles, which should make it easier to find the type of coping skill your client needs. It doesn't have to be read in order, instead you can pick the section or skill that fits your treatment plan and the needs and preferences of the client.

At the back of the book, I've included some crisis information for the U.S., Canada, the UK, and Australia. Also included in the back of the book are some of my favorite resources specifically for teens. I list helpful apps to track emotions and for relaxation, plus books, card decks, and other online resources for mindfulness, anxiety, stress, and anger.

Please feel free to copy and use any of the materials with anyone on your caseload. However, if another colleague wants to use the materials included in this book, please direct them to copingskillsforkids.com.

# INTRODUCTION

Hi! I'm Janine, a therapist who has been working with teens for 20 years, helping them manage their anxiety, their stress, their frustration, their sadness, and lots of other emotions. I love my job - it's fantastic when I see a client make amazing progress in managing their feelings, making good choices, and handling things that happen in their lives.

I became a therapist because I had a wonderful experience with therapy when I was a teenager. I was stressed out about a lot of things, dealing with friendship issues and family issues, and I needed support and guidance. I got that from my therapist. She helped me figure out what was going on, and together we worked on finding coping skills that worked for me. At some point during our work together, I realized that being a therapist was what I wanted to do with my life, too. It felt awesome to have an adult in my life who got me, and I wanted to do the same for other kids and teens.

Often during therapy, I spend a lot of time talking with my teen clients about the pressure, stress, and anxiety they are feeling. Here are some of the major themes that have come up regularly:

**School** - Tough classes, homework, concerns about grades or projects, conflicts with teachers, changing schools, challenging assignments, the impact grades can have on college applications, conflicts with classmates, teasing, and bullying.

**Family** - Fights with parents and/or siblings, arguments over rules, stressed out adults, parents getting separated or divorced, moving or living in multiple places, increased responsibilities at home like cleaning or caring for siblings or pets, family finances.

**Friendships** - Peer pressure, fights with friends, dating, changes in friendships, not having friends, or losing friends they did have, making or keeping plans, keeping up with what's happening on apps, group text messaging issues, feeling isolated or alone.

**Other stressors:** Finding a job, balancing work and school responsibilities, death of a loved one, higher expectations from the adults in their life.

Does any of this sound familiar to you?

Between schoolwork, college admissions pressure, worrying about what's going on social media, and conflicts with family or friends, it's no wonder teens overall are more stressed out and anxious these days. And it's hard to escape. If there's a huge fight happening with friends, just because you're not in the same space anymore

doesn't mean you can block out the argument. The fight can follow you via social

media or apps or on a group message.

Also, as a teen, your body and brain are experiencing a lot of changes. Your brain

develops and transforms SO MUCH as you go through adolescence. You'll also

experience puberty, which means a significant increase in hormones, which not

only impacts how your body is developing, but can also impact your emotions. Plus,

socially, things are changing for you. Friendships may be shifting and changing from

when you were younger, and you may start to get interested in dating or being in a

romantic relationship with someone.

Sometimes when you're faced with tough situations, or when you're experiencing

lots of emotions, you turn to unhealthy ways to cope. Sometimes you can do things

that are harmful, or unsafe, all in an effort to help manage your overwhelming

emotions. I want to tell you that you don't have to do this. You can make healthier

choices.

The truth is, you will feel a huge range of emotions as a teen and as you move into

adulthood. You probably experienced some pretty intense feelings when you were

younger, too. For example, you may experience incredible sadness, or unbelievable frustration, or righteous fury because of various things that happen in your life or in the world around you. Part of being human means that you will experience a wide variety of emotions throughout your week, your day, sometimes even within a few minutes.

I want to be clear that there is nothing wrong with being angry or worried or feeling any other emotion. Emotions aren't good or bad, they just are. What matters is what you do with those emotions. My wish for you is to be able to manage your emotions safely, in healthy ways, and in ways that aren't harmful to you, or anyone else.

Chances are, if you're reading this, you are looking for some help and support, and that's exactly why I wrote this book. I'm writing this workbook to give you some ideas of what you can do when things get stressful or overwhelming, or when you're feeling frustrated, angry, worried, anxious, sad, or anything else.

## The Science of Adolescence

When you are facing overwhelming feelings, sometimes it can help to understand how your body functions under stress.

To keep it simple, think of your brain as divided into two main parts: the emotional part of your brain and the rational part of your brain. The emotional part of your brain includes areas like the **brain stem** and **limbic system**. The brain stem is the part of the brain that takes in information, and regulates your breathing, eating, and digestion. The limbic system is the part of the brain that creates emotions, and is in charge of motivation. It is also the part of the brain where memories are created.

The rational part of your brain includes areas like the **temporal lobe** and **prefrontal cortex**. This is the part of the brain which helps you control impulses, think before you act, and make good decisions.

We can use with the hand model of the brain, which was created by Dr. Dan Siegel. It's a very simplified way to help us understand our brain and how it functions. Start by making a fist with your thumb inside.

Your emotional brain is represented by the palm of your hand and thumb, and your rational brain is represented by the fingers sitting on top of your thumb.

The human body is cool - there are some things that are done automatically for you by your **Autonomic Nervous System**; This system resides in the emotional part of your brain, and controls your breathing, your heart rate, your muscle tension, and your ability to digest food. There are two parts to the Autonomic Nervous System - the *parasympathetic* and the *sympathetic*.

Picture this: You're relaxed and nothing is bothering you. Your phone is fully charged and you finished your homework. Now you're binge watching the latest Netflix show...

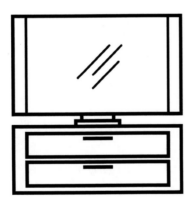

You are in "rest and digest" mode. The *parasympathetic* part of your Autonomic Nervous System is in charge, your breathing is slow and deep, your heart rate is within a normal range, your muscles aren't tense, and your body is digesting food normally.

But, now picture this: You get a text from a friend, reminding you that you have a test tomorrow, and you had forgotten all about it.

Now you're feeling anxious and stressed. Your body goes into "fight, flight, or freeze" mode. The *sympathetic* Autonomic System is taking over. That means that your breathing gets shallow, your heart rate goes up, your muscles get tense, and your digestion slows down. Basically, your body reacts like there is a real life dinosaur chasing you.

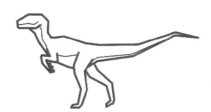

If we go back to the hand model of the brain, imagine that your fingers flip up, and suddenly the rational part of your brain is no longer in charge, instead it's the emotional part, which is much harder to reason with. Dr. Siegel calls this "flipping your lid."

This system was a great evolutionary tool, back in prehistoric days. It helped

humans deal with hunting/gathering, being chased by a predator, and managing

when there wasn't enough food to eat. Our bodies have held onto this adaptation

for centuries, and now, instead of activating when we're being chased, it activates

when we're stressed out or overwhelmed in school or with life. Same reaction,

different trigger.

As an adolescent, the part of your brain responsible for emotions grows a lot. That's

why you can feel so many emotions throughout the day. Your rational brain is also

developing more and more, and getting better at regulating your emotions,

problem solving, and thinking before you act; but it's not always smooth. The rush

of emotions and swift changes between tasks can feel overwhelming.

You may have heard adults tell you that teenagers' brains are still developing, as if

that's a bad thing. It's not an *easy* thing, for sure, but that doesn't make it bad. In fact, at this age, your brain is able to learn new things better than an adult's. As you learn and grow from what you experience, your brain takes on new information with greater skill and ease. So that makes this the perfect time to try healthy coping skills.

Why are we talking about all this, you might wonder. We're talking about it because there is power in knowing where your feelings come from. You can use that knowledge to manage your feelings. When you feel something, like worry, it can feel empowering to know you can do something about it. That worry doesn't have to stay with you forever. You can do something to make things better. This book has lots of coping skills you can use to help manage, express, and channel your feelings in healthier ways. Each skill has a little bit of a scientific explanation as to why it works. I want you to try them. You may feel stupid or think it's dumb. I get that. But what I always tell my clients, and what I'm asking you to do, is give it a shot. The worst that can happen is that you don't like it.

To make it easier to explore coping skills, the book is divided into coping styles. This makes it a little bit easier to find the type of coping skill that would be useful for you, depending on what you're feeling, where you are, and what you prefer. The coping strategies I've included are ones that I've tried with clients throughout the years that have worked well, or successful strategies that clients have shared with me.

The first section focuses on **Processing Coping Skills**, which are designed to help you identify what you are feeling, recognize the body signs of those feelings, and get an better understanding of your thoughts and emotions, and ideas to help you process those feelings in safe and healthy ways.

The second section has **Relaxation Coping Skills**. These are strategies you can use to work on the vital skill of taking deep breaths, exploring mindfulness, figuring out ways to relax your body and get calm when you need to.

The third section focuses on using **Movement and Sensory Coping Skills**. These strategies focus on using your body and your senses in different ways to help you manage your emotions.

The fourth section has **Distraction Coping Skills**. These are focused on having FUN! Play and leisure are natural stress relievers; everyone benefits when they take breaks and have a good time. Included in this section are some ideas of ways that you can chill out and give your brain a break.

Some strategies work better for certain emotions. For example, if you're experiencing anxiety, it may make sense to focus on relaxation strategies, especially deep breathing at first and then processing strategies. If you're dealing with anger, doing movement strategies may help you more. If you're trying to manage your stress levels, doing more processing around what's bothering you and stressing you out, and making a plan for next steps to reduce your stress levels makes more sense.

Also, keep in mind that different skills work better in certain locations. You can't necessarily make and listen to a playlist when you're in the middle of algebra, and you'll probably get in trouble just for having your phone out. A playlist would be a better skill to practice at home. However, something like 4-7-8 breathing -- a relaxation technique -- can work in the middle of class if you're starting to feel overwhelmed.

It's helpful to understand that coping skills can change over time. I often see with clients that what works at one time no longer works later, and what they didn't like before they now find helpful. I can even use myself as a perfect example of this. For years, I didn't do yoga. I have a hard time settling down my brain, and anytime I tried to do yoga, I found it frustrating. But then I lived in California for a year, and there were yoga classes happening all around me, at the gym, in parks, even at my next door neighbor's house. One day, I was feeling stressed and I was open to trying yoga. I went to class, and I actually felt better. I now try to do yoga regularly. But if you told me 10 years ago that I would do yoga, and actually find it pleasant, I would have laughed. Don't give up on any skill. Even if it doesn't work for you right now, it may work for you later on.

Because you need different coping skills to deal with different emotions, when you are in different places, or because of your own personal preference, it's good to explore every coping style to figure out what works best for you and helps you the most.

Some positive words clients have said about the coping skills I talk about this book are:

"I got through that presentation using that deep breathing strategy we tried!"

"My parents and I had a big talk about what's going on - writing that letter really helped me figure out what to say."

"I'm feeling better about things now than I did a few weeks ago - I've been hanging out with a friend and that's been fun."

In the **Wellness Worksheets** section of the book, you'll find a full list of the coping skills discussed that you can use to keep track of what does and doesn't work for you. Next to each coping skill, there are boxes where you can check off when you've tried it and if you liked it. This way you can keep track of what works for you, and just as importantly, what doesn't work for you right now. Then you can use the **Current Coping Skills** worksheet to quickly identify strategies you like. You can use these to create your **Self-Care Plan** for your different stressors, which is also in the back of the book.

This book is meant to help you but it is not a replacement for therapy, nor is it meant to help you manage a crisis situation. If you're not sure how to start seeking a therapist (or help in a crisis), I did want to give you some resources that might assist. At the back of the book, I've included some information on who you can call when you are in crisis in the U.S., Canada, the UK, and Australia. It is not an exhaustive list, but it could be a good place to start if you need help immediately.

You may need to work with an individual therapist to talk and explore your specific experiences. To make it a little easier, I have some suggestions about how to go about starting to look for a therapist in the back of the book. Also included in the back of the book are some of my favorite resources and tools. I list helpful apps to track emotions and for relaxation, plus books, card decks, and other online

resources for mindfulness, anxiety, stress, and anger.

# PART ONE: UNDERSTANDING AND PROCESSING YOUR THOUGHTS AND EMOTIONS

## "Feelings are mentionable and manageable."
## - Fred Rogers

Have you ever had one of those days where your emotions are all over the place? One minute you're happy, then you're sad, then frustrated, then anxious, then happy again. It can be overwhelming, making it difficult to manage everyday tasks. It can also make you feel like maybe there's something wrong with you. But it's normal to experience a wide variety of emotions during a day, or even during a few moments. It can be helpful to learn how to manage those emotions in a healthy, calm way, and that's what this book can help you do.

The first step in being able to manage your emotions is to know what they are. And remember, like I said in the introduction, feelings are not good or bad, they just are. It is okay for you to feel frustrated, sad, anxious, worried, scared, uncertain, etc. It's what you do with those emotions that matters the most.

It's also really helpful for you to be able to identify what caused those different feelings, and how to express those feelings in ways that won't harm you or others around you.

In this section, there are 15 coping skills focused on different ways to identify and express your feelings. The first few focus on recognizing your feelings and what situations are more challenging for you. The next few skills focus on your thoughts and inner dialogue, then the last several strategies focus on ways you can express your emotions to get it out in safe ways.

# 1. Identify Your Feelings

Everyone feels emotions at one time or another. Your teachers, your parents, your church leaders, your coaches, or your little siblings all feel emotions. Researchers like Dr. Paul Ekman and Dr. Robert Plutchik explored **universal feelings**, or feelings that everyone has and demonstrates. Dr. Ekman identified six basic emotions (anger, disgust, fear, happiness, sadness, and surprise). Dr. Plutchik identified eight, which he grouped into four pairs of polar opposites (joy-sadness, anger-fear, trust-distrust, surprise-anticipation). In addition, research has found that we can also recognize those emotions in others because they all use very similar facial expressions.

Why should we bother labelling our feelings? Clinical research has demonstrated that one way to help you learn how to regulate your emotions is to identify them. In other words, once you can identify your emotions, it becomes easier to manage them. As Dr. Dan Siegel says, "When you name it, you can tame it."

So where should you begin? Start by tracking how you feel on a regular basis. See the worksheet on the next page designed to make it easier for you to track your feelings.

## Date & Time                                          ## Feelings

_____  Happy  Sad  Angry  Worried  Frustrated  Scared  _____

_____  Happy  Sad  Angry  Worried  Frustrated  Scared  _____

_____  Happy  Sad  Angry  Worried  Frustrated  Scared  _____

_____  Happy  Sad  Angry  Worried  Frustrated  Scared  _____

_____  Happy  Sad  Angry  Worried  Frustrated  Scared  _____

_____  Happy  Sad  Angry  Worried  Frustrated  Scared  _____

_____  Happy  Sad  Angry  Worried  Frustrated  Scared  _____

_____  Happy  Sad  Angry  Worried  Frustrated  Scared  _____

_____  Happy  Sad  Angry  Worried  Frustrated  Scared  _____

_____  Happy  Sad  Angry  Worried  Frustrated  Scared  _____

_____  Happy  Sad  Angry  Worried  Frustrated  Scared  _____

_____  Happy  Sad  Angry  Worried  Frustrated  Scared  _____

_____  Happy  Sad  Angry  Worried  Frustrated  Scared  _____

_____  Happy  Sad  Angry  Worried  Frustrated  Scared  _____

Notice on this worksheet there is space for you to add other feelings as well, not just the six basic ones I listed. Feel free to write in your own. My recommendation is to start by tracking your feelings at least once a day, but you can also track your feelings more frequently if you desire. Some ideas:

- in the morning and at night

- before school, after school, and before bed

Also, it's okay if you circle more than one feeling at a check-in time. You can feel a lot of different ways through the course of a typical day, there's nothing wrong with that.

If you prefer, you can use an app to track your feelings instead. A few out there that may work for you include:

- **The Mood Meter App** - Designed based on decades of research out of Yale, with reminders to help you keep track of what you are feeling.

- **Daylio** - A mood tracking where you don't have to use words, you can instead visually select your feeling.

- **MoodKit** - Developed by clinical psychologists, this app lets you track your moods and see them on a chart. This app also offers ideas for helping you manage emotions. You can use it as a journal as well.

# 2. Recognize Feelings in Your Body

Your body gives you clues as to what you are feeling. A recent research study found that certain feelings can be associated with sensations in different parts of your body. For example, you may feel anger in your head and upper body and arms, you may feel happiness all over your body, or you may feel sad in your legs and arms.

If you are struggling to figure out what you are feeling, you can use the clues that your body, mind, and actions are giving you. You can be a detective, take those hints and help you decipher the message.

## Clues from Your Body

Let's start with your body. Think about how different parts of your body feel. How does your head feel? Your neck? Arms? Hands? Stomach? Legs? Feet?

Here are some ways I've had clients describe different feelings in relation to their bodies:

## Anger

"feeling heat rise on my neck and face, and my hands clench"

"feeling twitchy in my legs like I want to run"

"my heart feels like it's going to burst"

## Worry

"tingling on my arms and legs"

"rolling in my stomach"

"my head feels dizzy"

## Sadness

"my eyes start to water, and I can't stop it"

"my legs feel so heavy, and it's hard to move"

"my mind goes foggy"

## Clues from your mind

Sometimes your thoughts can give you clues as to how you may be feeling. Write down what thoughts are going through your head and see if that helps give you any more clues.

"Everyone keeps talking about tests and grades and getting into college, and it's boring and annoying." What could this tell you about how you're feeling? Maybe you're feeling anxious that you're not going to measure up and get into the school you want.

"She's supposed to be my friend, but she just walked past me and didn't say anything!" What could this tell you about how you're feeling? Maybe you're worried that she might be angry with you, distrustful that she is really the friend you thought she was, hurt that she didn't treat you as you expect to be treated, or even angry at *her* about this, or something else.

## Clues from your actions

Another clue is how you act. Are you noticing changes that are different than how you normally act? Some things you might notice include:

- Changes in appetite

- Sleeping more or less than usual

- Fidgeting more

- Difficulty concentrating

- Losing interest in things you typically love doing

- Isolating yourself

If you find that these changes have lasted more than a couple of weeks, it may mean that you are dealing with a bigger mental health concern. This is when it's important to tell an adult you trust about what you've noticed, so they can help support you and get you more help if you need it.

To make it easier to keep track of the clues from your body, your mind, and your actions, there's a worksheet you can use on the next page.

# Recognizing Feelings

## Body

## Mind

## Actions

# 3. Be prepared! Identifying Challenging Situations

There are lots of situations that can cause you to feel overwhelmed, anxious, stressed, or angry. Sometimes this can happen out of the blue - you didn't anticipate it, and you're trying to deal with it in the moment. However, for a lot of people, there are certain situations that happen over and over to cause them to feel stressed or overwhelmed. If you know what those situations are, then when you are faced with one of those events in the future, you can make a plan and prepare yourself ahead of time.

When you know what might be a challenging situation, you can plan better for it.

For instance, if midterms week tends to be a very stressful time, you can be as thoughtful as possible when it comes planning your study and work schedules. You can look at your schedule the week or two before midterms and add in early studying so that you don't get overwhelmed when the time comes. You can also plan some extra downtime or stress-relieving activities during this period, since you know it will be a hard time.

Keep in mind that it is just as important to make sure there are things you are NOT doing at this stressful time. If midterms stress you out, and planning a party stresses you out, don't plan any big social events during this already stressful time.

Use the worksheet on the next page to identify things that set you off (otherwise known as "triggers"), and things you can do to deal with those triggers in a healthy way.

# Identify Triggers and Make a Plan

| Triggers | What's the Plan? |
| --- | --- |
| | |

# 4. Acknowledge What You Can and Can't Control

One of the biggest lessons I learned when I was in therapy as a teen was to acknowledge what I can and can't control. You want your friends to want to see the same movie you want to see. You want your crush to like you back. You want your parents to change their minds and let you do the thing you really want to do. But the problem is, you have no control over other people.

Let me clarify a little bit - your behaviors impact other people, and that may influence how they behave. Have you ever heard the saying "You get more bees with honey?" If you act in a certain way, it's more likely that people will respond positively to you. Your behaviors and how you act can have an impact on others, but it's not a guarantee.

Instead of focusing on what others are doing, you can focus on what you CAN control, and that is YOU. You can control how you act, what you say, what you do, how you behave, how you respond to someone. And those things do influence how someone responds to you.

So, it's best to focus on what you do have control over, and that is yourself. When you are in a situation with another person who is making you mad, you can control how you react to them, what you say, etc. When you are dealing with a frustrating teacher, you can control what you say and what you do, but you can't control their response. Here's a visual to help you understand the things you do have control over and the things you don't have control over in your life.

**What would you add to this?**

**What I can't control**

other people's behaviors

other people's actions

**What I can control**

my words
my actions
my behaviors
how I respond

the weather

other people's feelings

decisions made by the adults in your life (job change, moving, etc)

# 5. Identify Thinking Errors

# You Don't Have to Believe Every Thought That Crosses Your

# Mind!

There are lots of thoughts that cross your mind every day. Some are good and positive, and can be encouraging, but others aren't helpful. When you are having a hard time or facing tough situations, you can have thoughts that are not true to reality. These thoughts are called **thinking errors**, and they can make you feel horrible about yourself.

But if you can recognize these negative thoughts as thinking errors, you can remind yourself that just because you think something negative doesn't mean it's true. You don't have to believe every thought that comes through your head.

Let's explore a few of those unhelpful thinking errors with a couple of examples:

**All or Nothing Thinking** - Seeing things in only two categories - all good or all bad - without noticing or acknowledging the fuzzy gray areas in life.

For example: "Life is perfect!" or "Life is terrible."

You don't have to believe this. Instead, let's try reframing this thinking error.

Reframe:

"The truth is life is full of gray areas! There are some things in life that are good, some things in life that aren't so good, and some that are kind of neutral."

**Jumping to Conclusions** - Assuming that something is true without actual facts and information to back that up.

For example: "They were making a funny face when they looked at me. That must mean they can't stand me and don't want to be my friend anymore."

Let's reframe this one:

"Maybe my friend was about to sneeze. Or they were thinking about something gross. Just because a person has a funny look on their face doesn't mean they don't want to be my friend."

**Catastrophizing** - Making small issues into a really big deal.

For example: "I failed my math test. I'm not going to pass math this year, and I won't be able to get into the college I want, or get a good job."

Reframe:

"The reality is that it's one math test. One math test won't determine the rest of my life, even though it may feel that way right now."

**<u>Overgeneralization</u>** - Making a rule about yourself or life based on a couple of experiences you have.

For instance, one speech in front of the class does not go well, and then you have decided that "I'm not a good public speaker, I never will be, and all my future speeches will be horrible too."

Reframe:

"One bad speech doesn't mean I'll always be awful at it. I can learn from this, and make changes for the next time."

When you find yourself having these thoughts, the first thing to do is to label it as a thinking error, then try to reframe it. Recognize that the negative thoughts aren't always true, and remember that you don't have to believe everything you think.

# 6. Change Your Inner Dialogue

## "Talk to yourself like you would to someone you love."
## - Brene Brown

A lot of thoughts cross your mind during the day. You may notice that some are more positive thoughts, and some are negative. Now you know what thinking errors are, you may be able to identify those negative thoughts more easily. The next thing you want to do is work on changing the script. It's almost like those negative thoughts are a playlist in your head. They say the same negative unhelpful things over and over until you can't get them out of your mind. So, let's work on changing the playlist!

Sometimes people identify thoughts that are positive as **green thoughts** or helpful thoughts, and identify negative thoughts as harmful or **red thoughts**. You can call them whatever you want. No matter what you call them, we want to change those negative thoughts into more positive ones. You can see some examples of changing negative thoughts to more positive ones on the next page.

Research has found that it's beneficial to use your own name when you're talking to yourself and trying to encourage yourself with more positive thoughts. Talk to yourself like you would talk to your best friend if they were having a hard time. After all, if you aren't treating yourself with the same forgiving and generous spirit you treat your friends, then you aren't giving yourself the best chance to support yourself.

Let's practice changing those negative thoughts into more positive, realistic thoughts. See the chart below for a couple of examples. Plus, there's a worksheet you can fill in yourself with your own negative thoughts and rewrite them into more positive thoughts.

| **Negative Self -Talk**<br>Write down those negative thoughts in your head. | **Positive Self-Talk**<br>Change those negatives into positives. Use your own name when you're writing the sentences! |
|---|---|
| I can't do this.... | Janine, you can't do this *yet*, but you can work hard and try again. |
| I'm never going to get into college, I'm too stupid... | Janine, be kind to yourself. |

# Changing Negative Self-Talk to Positive Self- Talk

## Negative Self -Talk

Write down those negative thoughts in your head.

## Positive Self-Talk

Change those negatives into positives. Use your own name when you're writing the sentences!

# 7. Make a Plan to Solve a Problem

Do you ever get worried or stressed when you have a problem - like when you have to give a class presentation and you don't feel ready? Or you have to go somewhere new and you're nervous? Or when you and a friend are in a fight? While it's tough to think about these worries, it's good to try to get to the bottom of what's going on and make a plan for what you can do to solve it. Ignoring a problem usually won't make it go away. Instead, try to tackle it and figure out what you can do to make the situation better. For example, let's say you and your friend are in a fight. You have NO IDEA what to do.

## Identify the Problem

The first step is to identify the problem you are having. The problem is "I'm in this huge fight with my best friend and I don't even understand why this is happening."

## Generate Ideas

The next step is to generate several ideas for solving an issue. Not all of them will work, but you're not trying to pick out ones that will and won't work during this step. Right now, it's just about generating ideas.

For example:

- Ask a mutual friend what happened

- Tell her she's rude and that she needs to talk to me

- Never speak to her again

- Send her a text and say I want to talk

- Talk to her in homeroom before school begins

- Talk with her at my house

## Pick out the good ideas for solving the problem and use them!

Sometimes seeing your ideas written down can help you pick the best option. For example, it may not be the best idea to involve others in the argument, or to talk in a public place like the hallway at school. Nor will you make a problem better by calling her rude and telling her what to do, or choosing to never talk to her again.

Here's a plan that might work better: "I'm going to send her a text and say that I noticed she's upset and I want to talk with her. I'll invite her over to my house after school so we can talk privately. "

Now you have a plan to help you manage this new situation. You can use these steps to help you identify problems and generate solutions when you're worried about something.

If you're having a problem figuring out which solutions would be helpful and which would make it worse, then ask a family member, a school counselor or other trusted adult, or someone else who is not involved with this issue at all. Usually when you ask others for help, you can get ideas you would never think of yourself. Then you can decide what to do.

# 8. Think About the Best Thing That Could Happen

When you are worried or stressed or anxious about an upcoming event, it's very easy to think of all the bad things that could happen. You fall into the worst case scenario rabbit hole, and think of all the horrible things that may occur. For example, say you just met a new friend at an after-school thing, and you made plans to go out for coffee after.

You may think to yourself:

*"I'm going to hang out with my new friend at the coffee shop and I'm worried that it will be terrible. I'm going to say something stupid or say something the wrong way, then he'll never speak to me again and start spreading rumors that I'm an idiot and I'll lose all my other friends too!"*

Often we get stuck focusing on all the things that could go wrong, but it usually doesn't end up that way. There are usually some good things that happen too. Once you're done thinking of all the things that could go wrong, switch it up. Ask yourself what is the best case scenario?

You may think to yourself:

"We could discover we both love the same band."

"It could go really well, and then we hang out again next week."

"If I say something silly, we can turn it into an inside joke!"

So the next time you are facing an uncertain situation and you're starting to fall into the worst case scenario, take a moment and list all of the good things that could happen instead!

## 9. Express What You're Feeling in a Creative Way

**"I found I could say things with colors and shapes that I couldn't say in any other way - things that I had no words for."**

**- Georgia O'Keeffe**

I once worked with this 17-year-old who was almost a foot taller than me, and was dealing with anxiety and depression. He said that the only thing that really helped him was his music. He wrote raps and music lyrics, and created the melodies that went along with it. He would show me what he was working on, or play something for me, and we talked all the time about how he felt better, like something had released, when he wrote it down. We talked about musical artists who used their experiences and their emotions as inspiration for their work. Expressing yourself in a creative way is a fantastic outlet to get out some of the things you're feeling without words.

There is a ton of research about the positive impact that using art and music can have on helping young people manage their emotions and reduce stress.

Here are some ideas for creatively expressing yourself:

- Writing a book, or short story, or graphic novel

- Composing music

- Writing poems or raps

- Dancing - either freestyle, or making up choreography

- Singing - songs or melodies you've heard and love, or make up your own

- Painting - you can try different mediums and canvases

- Drawing, sketching, or doodling

## 10. Channel Big Emotions into Positive Action

"Never doubt that a small group of thoughtful, committed citizens can change the world; indeed, it's the only thing that ever has."

\- Margaret Mead

There are a lot of things that happen in the world that can make us really angry. Some people just sit and let that anger fester, but anger can actually be a great motivator to make change. Change sometimes happens when people get fed up with how things are, and then they work together to do something positive for the world.

Lady Gaga has used music and acting as a way to help her cope with the bullying, anxiety, and depression that she dealt with growing up. She was able to find a way to express her real self, which led to her success and the ability to inspire young people who are dealing with similar experiences.

Bikers against Bullies was founded in Missoula, Montana by a dad whose child was being bullied for being different. He got angry, then he created a group to help other kids who have been bullied, and started riding his motorcycle into schools to talk about his experiences and encourage kind and respect behaviors to everyone.

Young people today are using their anger and frustration and working to make a change. Even as a teen, you can have an impact. Teens like Greta Thunberg and Alexandria Villaseñor got angry about global warming. They've organized protests and started groups like Youth Climate Strike and Earth Uprising to make people more aware of these issues and make changes to do something to protect the future.

*"I get angry over injustice. I think a lot of young people do. It's like we can naturally see when something is hurting someone, and so we speak out. As people grow up they look away and most of them don't get angry anymore. I watched Greta Thunberg give her speech at COP 24, and everything she said was right. Then the adults, like, figuratively patted her on the head and kept right on burning fossil fuels. That made me angry, and that is when I decided to act on climate change. When I went on strike I didn't understand what being an activist was. I just knew I was angry about what was happening to our planet." - Alexandria Villaseñor*

People used their anger, their frustration, their aggravation, and their experiences and channeled that into helpful positive action. If you find yourself getting mad about the same things over and over again, is there something you can do to make a bigger impact?

# 11. Get Your Feelings Out on Paper

When I worked in a middle school, I had a certain student who got especially frustrated with his math teacher. This student would sometimes get into trouble for arguing back, or being disrespectful. We worked on holding his tongue and waiting to express what he wanted to say in a different format. He would come to my office, and write down what he wished he could say to that teacher. Then he would scribble on top of it, and rip up the paper and throw it away. He was still able to express his thoughts and feelings, but he did it in a way that wasn't going to earn him a detention or more time after school with this same teacher he didn't get along with. It seemed to help him get out his frustrations in a way that did not get him into any more trouble, and also gave him a chance to share his true, raw thoughts and feelings.

You can do this yourself by:

- Writing down in words or phrases things that are bothering you

- Writing what you wish you could say

- Scribbling to express your emotions. You can even have different colors for different emotions (red = angry, orange = frustrated, purple = scared, blue = anxious)

Next, figure out what you want to do with what you just did, you could:

- paint over it

- rip it up

- put black marker over everything you did

- shred it

- ball it up and throw it away

There are times when it would be beneficial to share your feelings. For instance, if a friend did something that really made you angry, or you want to express your emotions to your parents about a particular situation.

Get your feelings out on paper, and then spend a little time thinking about how you want to approach the situation. Use the steps in **Make a Plan to Solve the Problem** from earlier in this chapter to help you make a plan for what to do and how to approach the situation in the best way possible.

While it may be tempting to share your thoughts and feelings on social media, I would caution against that. Once you've put something out there, you no longer control it. Instead, focus on writing on real paper, or places where it won't be broadcast to all your followers or can come up in a search on an app.

# 12. Write in a Journal

Whenever I sit down and talk with someone about their coping skills, one of the first things I ask is: "Have you tried writing about it?" I encourage people to write things down all the time. There are a bunch of reasons why this works.

## It's easier to write about hard things than it is to talk about hard things.

These are your personal private thoughts. If your journal is private and you feel comfortable that no one will read what you write, then you are free to say everything you really feel - the good, the bad, and the horrible stuff you'd never say out loud.

## Journaling can help you process what's happening around you

When you write, you mull over things in your head, and it sometimes helps you come to new realizations about the issues you are dealing with at the present time. It can also help you understand past issues in a different way.

## It's convenient

It's always available because it's portable. You can take your journal anywhere. All you need is a place to write and a pen or pencil. Or if you want to, you can also use a computer. Sometimes people write in the notes section on their phone, or on an ipad or laptop. That's also portable and convenient.

## It's not graded

You don't have to use perfect grammar. You don't even need to use full sentences. You can just write phrases, words, or statements. Write whatever helps you work through things.

## It can help you solve a problem

Sometimes through writing, you can think outside the box, or consider different strategies for solving a problem you hadn't thought of before. If you're struggling to figure something out, writing may help you come up with another idea to try.

## It can help you re-frame your thinking

Writing can help you focus on the positives, too. Sometimes, it can help to write down three things you are grateful for, or write down three things that went well during the past day or week. This is especially helpful if you have been writing about difficult experiences. End the writing session by focusing on the positives. Use the **Journal** page on the next page to start your own journaling process. Copy it as many times as you need!

# Journal

_____

_____

_____

_____

_____

_____

_____

_____

_____

_____

_____

_____

_____

_____

## Positives from the day

_____

_____

_____

_____

# 13. Write a Letter You Never Send

There are times you are feeling some big emotions towards someone else, but for whatever reason, you can't or don't want to communicate directly to them. What you can do is write them a letter. Similar to journaling, this can be a cathartic experience. Getting your thoughts and feelings out on paper or in a digital format can be amazingly helpful. You know you're not sending it out to them, so you can say all the things you really wish you could, but wouldn't necessarily say out loud because it may be too hurtful or rude.

This exercise is a good way to get all your emotions out around a certain experience, especially if it's been hard to figure out and there have been a ton of complications and feelings around it. If you plan on trying to talk with this person again, you can use the letter as a way to figure out exactly what you do want to say to them. You never have to share the letter with them but it's a helpful way to process and organize your thoughts around tough situations.

In some situations, you may be writing a letter to someone who you're no longer speaking to. Writing this letter could be a way to put closure on a situation for yourself. You can express your thoughts and emotions about what went wrong, and share your final thoughts. This is a way you can move forward in your life.

# 14. Use the Power of Music

## "After silence, that which comes nearest to expressing the inexpressible is music."

## - Aldous Huxley

Has a song ever filled you with happiness and joy so that you can't help but sing and dance? Have you ever had strong memories come flooding back when you hear a certain song? Have you ever cried when listening to a piece of music? If so, then you have experienced the power of music. Music has the power to change people's moods. It can take someone from feeling sad to feeling happy. It can energize you. It can move you to the point of tears.

You can help yourself by creating playlists for specific moods. First, figure out what you are currently feeling. Then ask yourself you'd like to be feeling and thinking instead. Make multiple playlists for whatever you'd like to feel, and name them accordingly. For instance:

- If you are feeling sad, perhaps you want to make a playlist full of songs that make you smile.

- If you are feeling helpless, make a playlist of songs that makes you feel strong.

- If you are feeling like you have no energy, make a playlist of songs that makes you want to get up and do something.

# 15. Defeat Your Worry

Sometimes dealing with anxiety and worry can feel like a battle. It feels like you're in a constant fight and it seems like you don't have any control. One thing that helps is to give your anxiety a name. Here are a couple of examples:

- "the bully"

- "the worry machine"

- "the fear causer"

Once you give it a name, then you can directly address it. When those thoughts start to impact you, then you can talk to it, and control your reaction to it. You can talk back to your anxiety, your worry or your fear. You can say,

- "I don't have to believe you!"

- "Stop your nonsense."

- "Cut it out."

- "Just because you say it doesn't make it true!"

It may help to visualize this process of you talking back to your anxiety. Use the worksheet on the next page to help you defeat your anxiety.

First, draw your anxiety. It doesn't have to look like a person, it could be a splotch of color, or a shape, or a weird spiky thing. You can even write the name you've given your anxiety on that page.

*Name: "fear causer"*

Next draw your anxiety being defeated. You could draw yourself, big and strong, with a shield and a sword. Or you could draw a powerful storm that blows your anxiety away.  Or an army defeating your anxiety. Or trap your anxiety in a bubble. You could even write the words you might say back to your "fear causer."

# Defeat Your Anxiety

In the box below, draw your anxiety. Once you're done depicting your anxiety, then draw it getting defeated. Ideas to defeat your anxiety: a protective shield, an army or a powerful storm that comes in and washes it away.

# PART TWO: RELAXATION AND MINDFULNESS TECHNIQUES

Never in the history of calming down has anyone calmed down by being told to calm down.

- Dr. Ross Greene

"Just calm down."

How annoying is that? How often has someone said that to you, expecting you to actually calm down? When you're having a moment, it's hard to "just calm down." If you *could* calm down, you would. Coming up in this next section are some strategies that you can use so that you can calm down and relax when things are starting to feel overwhelming.

Just a reminder, that even though it seems silly, deep breathing matters. Remember breathing is part of your Autonomic Nervous System, which controls your heart rate, digestion, tension in your muscles, and breathing. When you are calm and relaxed, your autonomic system is in rest-and-digest mode, which means your heart rate is normal, your digestion is normal, and you're breathing deeply. When you get overwhelmed or in a state of anxiety or extreme worry, your autonomic nervous system goes into fight, flight, or freeze, which means your heart starts to race, your digestion slows down, and your breathing gets shallow. Deep breathing is a way to tell your body it's time to switch back to rest and digest mode. The first few strategies in this section are all about deep breathing. Then I share some other helpful relaxation techniques for you to try.

# 1. Take a Deep Breath Using your Hand

So, I'm sure you have been told to take deep breaths a number of ways, but truthfully, I know you don't want anyone to see what you're doing. This strategy is one you can do in class, and people don't even have to know that you're doing it.

To take deep breaths with your hand: breathe in and trace the outside of your thumb, breathe out and trace the inside of your thumb. Keep going with each finger - when you're done, you've taken five deep breaths.

You can put your hand on your lap under your desk so no one can really see what you're doing. If someone happens to look over, it just looks like you're tracing your hand - people won't know that you're using a coping skill.

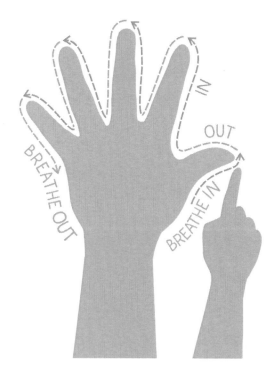

# 2. Take Deep Breaths using Numbers

You can use numbers to help yourself take deep breaths. Here are two of my favorite breathing strategies using numbers.

**Count to 10 Breathing:** Breathe in and out using each number to help give you a framework for taking deep breaths. Here's how to do it:

Inhale ONE    Exhale TWO

        Inhale THREE    Exhale FOUR

           Inhale FIVE    Exhale SIX

        Inhale SEVEN    Exhale EIGHT

Inhale NINE    Exhale TEN

**4 - 7 - 8 Breathing:** If you're in a state of panic, try 4 - 7 - 8 breathing. Breathe in for 4 counts, hold your breath for 7 counts, then breathe out for 8 counts. This strategy comes from yoga practice, and is designed to help you calm down. The longer breath out helps your heart rate slow down more because when you exhale, your heartbeat is naturally a little slower.

# 3. Use Technology to Take a Deep Breath

I love using technology in ways that can help you take deep breaths. You can keep gifs on your phone that encourage deep breathing. If you have a smart watch or a Fitbit, sometimes they will have a setting that can help you take deep breaths. The watch vibrates to alert you to take several deep breaths in and out. And the best thing is that no one has to know that you are using it!

Here is a collection of apps that you can use to help you take deep breaths:

- Relax Stress & Anxiety Relief

- Calm

- Headspace

- Insight Timer

- Breathing Zone

*Please note: While all of these apps are available on Apple App Store and Google Play at the time of this publication, this may change.*

If you visit my YouTube channel, in the Coping Skills for Teens playlist, you'll find some gifs and videos to help you take deep breaths.

# 4. Be Mindful

Mindfulness is quite a popular topic these days. Some schools are making mindfulness part of the day, or even replacing detentions with mindful practices. But what does that even mean? And how exactly do you do it?

## What is Mindfulness?

Put in the simplest terms, mindfulness is being aware of what's happening in the present moment. It's not about trying to clear your mind, but allowing thoughts and emotions to come and go without judgment and familiarizing ourselves with the present moment. Other words and phrases that have been used to describe mindfulness are:

- "concentration and attention"

- "loving presence"

- "awareness"

- "seeing clearly"

Mindfulness helps you focus on the present instead of focusing on the past or future. When you are aware of the present, it will help you be more able to see what's happening around you and settle yourself and your mind. It takes practice to be able to do this.

You don't have to do meditation and mindfulness for long to feel the effects. It can be done in 5 or 10 minutes. Regular meditation has been shown to shrink the **amygdala**, which is responsible for those big emotional reactions in your brain.

Here is a simple way to start:

- Take a minute, and focus on what you hear. The clock ticking? Cars outside? Birds chirping?

- Take another minute, and really look at where you are. Notice shapes, colors, try to find things you never noticed before.

- Take one more minute and focus on how your body feels. Do you feel a little hungry? Do you feel sore? Are you tired?

You can pay attention to what's going on around you any time. You can do this while walking, in between classes, when you wake up, or when you're falling asleep.

Sometimes, people even eat in a mindful way, paying attention to what their food looks like before they eat it, and focusing on all the sensory parts of eating, what it tastes like and feels like as they chew bite by bite. Some good foods to start with are chocolate, raspberries, or blackberries. It's a great way to get started on paying attention to what you are doing in the moment!

*Please be careful of food allergies. If you know you're allergic to it, or have had a bad reaction to something in the past, please don't eat it without consulting your doctor or allergist first.*

# 5. Do a Progressive Muscle Relaxation

Progressive Muscle Relaxation (PMR) is one of my favorite strategies for relaxation. It is also the one I've been using the longest. I remember doing this as part of one of my first ever Psych 101 classes in college, and I fell in love with the strategy. PMR means contracting and relaxing muscles in your body, with the goal of leaving your entire body relaxed.

There are tons of scripts out there that you can read to help you focus on different sections of your body. You can have someone read the script below to you to help you relax. There is a video version of this script on YouTube - visit the Coping Skills for Teens playlist to watch it.

*Dim the lights and turn off any screens. Sit down or lie down in a comfortable position. When you feel comfortable, close your eyes. During this exercise, you'll be instructed to tighten muscles. If you feel uncomfortable, take a break and focus on your breathing.*

*Let's start by taking some deep breaths. Breathe in and have your belly expand like a balloon. Breathe out and have your belly contract like air is leaving the balloon. Take another breath in and breathe out. Breathe in and breathe out.*

*Focus on the muscles in your face. Pretend you smell something really terrible, and wrinkle your nose and scrunch all the muscles in your face. Now let your muscles relax. That smell came back, wrinkle your nose and scrunch up your face again. Let your face relax. One more time, the smell is back - wrinkle and scrunch. Let your face relax.*

*Let's move on to your shoulders. Pull up your shoulders almost to your earlobes and tighten your shoulder muscles. Release and let your shoulders fall back down. Tighten your shoulders to your ears again. Then release. One more time, pull your shoulders to your ears. Then release.*

*Now, let's concentrate on your hands. Pretend you have two huge pieces of play dough in your hands and you need to squeeze it. Squeeze your hands and squish the play dough. Then let your hands relax. Squeeze the play dough again, then relax. Once more squeeze the play dough, then relax.*

*Next, let's pretend you are trying to squeeze through a small hole. Take a deep breath in then breathe out and squeeze your belly tight so you can get through. You're making your way through this small spot. Take another deep breath in, then breathe out and squeeze your belly tight. You're almost there! Take another deep breath in, then breathe out and squeeze your belly tight.*

*Now pretend like you are standing in sand and you want to make deep footprints. Press down hard into the sand.Keep going. Relax and move your feet. Now let's make another set of footprints. Press down hard. Relax and move your feet again. One more time, let's make this set of footprints super deep. Now relax and move your feet.*

*Relax and take another few deep breaths. The relaxation exercise is almost over. Slowly start to move your body and open your eyes when you feel ready.*

**Once you've done this exercise, check in with yourself. How do you feel? Do you feel more relaxed than you did a few minutes ago?**

# 6. Do a Body Scan

A body scan is a way to go through your body and pay attention to the sensations to see how your body feels. It's also an alternative to try if PMR doesn't feel good to you. Instead of tensing the muscle groups, you focus on them and try to let the tension release from the muscles. You can have someone read the script below to you to help you relax. Or you can visit the YouTube Coping Skills for Teens playlist for a video version of this script.

*Lay down or sit in a chair, and close your eyes.*

*Start with a few slow deep breaths. Breathe in, and breathe out.*

*As we go through the different muscle groups in your body, imagine that there is a light focused on that particular part of your body. When the light or warmth is focused on a part of your body, then let that part of your body relax.*

*Let's begin at the top of your body. Focus on the muscles in your face. Do you feel any tension? As you breathe out, let the muscles in your face relax. Keep taking deep breaths in and out, and as you exhale, feel the muscles relax more each time.*

*Next, let's move on to your neck. How does your neck feel? Focus the light on your neck, and as you breathe out, let the muscle tension relax. With each exhale, your muscles will release more tension.*

*Let's focus on your shoulders next. How do they feel? As you breathe out, let your muscles in your shoulders relax. You may notice that you've been holding your shoulders higher; if so, lower them down. Keep taking deep breaths in and out, and as you exhale, feel the muscles relax more each time.*

*Now let's focus on your back. How does your back feel? Focus the light on your back, and as you breathe out, let the tension in your muscles melt away. Keep taking a few deep breaths, and feel the muscles relax more each time.*

*Let's focus on your stomach now. How does it feel? Focus the light there, and see how your stomach feels. Keep taking deep breaths in and out, and as you exhale, feel the muscles relax more each time.*

*Now let's focus on your hips. Is there tension there? Focus the light on your hips and take deep breaths. With each exhale, feel your muscles relax.*

*Let's focus on your legs next. Focus the light on your legs. How do they feel? As you take deep breaths, allow the tension to melt away from your muscles.*

*Finally, let's focus on your feet. How do your feet feel? Focus the light there, and continue to take deep breaths. Allow the tension to melt away from your body.*

*Now focus on your whole body. Imagine there is a light focused on your whole body. Does your body feel different from when we started?*

*Keep taking a few more deep breaths. When you are ready, you can open your eyes, as you get ready to return to the world, feeling more relaxed and calmer.*

**Once you've done this exercise, check in with yourself.  How do you feel? Do you feel more relaxed than you did a few minutes ago?**

## 7. Make a Gratitude List

**It's not happiness that makes us grateful, it's gratefulness that makes us happy.**

**- Brother David Steindl-Rast**

There are a lot of famous people like Arianna Huffington, Oprah, and Deepak Chopra who are talking about gratefulness. There's also a lot of research around gratitude, which shows that being grateful can improve psychological health, reduce toxic emotions, and increase empathy.

What can you do to start focusing on gratitude and reaping these benefits? You can take a few minutes every week, and write down a few things you are thankful for. If you find it challenging at first, focus on just 2 or 3 things you are grateful for.

It doesn't have to be big. It could be that you're grateful for how the sun feels on your skin, or that your friend makes you laugh, or that your mom made your favorite breakfast. It could be that you're able to fall asleep easily one night after you've been struggling with sleeping. Or it could be big things, like you're grateful for your family, people who love you, or your support system.

You can write them on a slip of paper, and put them in a jar. That way you can physically see all the things you are thankful for. Or you could take strips of paper and make a paper chain of gratitude that you hang in your room. Or you can write it in a journal. On the next page, you'll find a Gratitude List to get you started.

**Date**                              **Things I'm grateful for**

_____        _____

_____        _____

_____        _____

_____        _____

_____        _____

_____        _____

_____        _____

_____        _____

_____        _____

_____        _____

_____        _____

_____        _____

_____        _____

_____        _____

_____        _____

_____        **Things I'm grateful for**

# 8. Go Through 54321 Grounding

What on earth is a **grounding** technique? Grounding is just a fancy way of saying "focus on the present moment." Using your five senses is a helpful way to focus on what's happening around you right in the present moment. This calming technique can help you get through tough or stressful situations. I first heard about it from another client, and since then, I have been sharing it with my own clients as a strategy to use when they are overwhelmed.

For instance, I had one client who was experiencing a ton of anxiety as she was running errands with her family, and I suggested that she try this one. It worked very well for her to help her calm down and get through the things she and her family needed to accomplish that day.

Take a deep belly breath to begin.

5 - LOOK: Look around for FIVE things that you can see, and say them out loud. For example, you could say, I see the computer, I see the cup, I see the picture frame.

4 - FEEL: Pay attention to your body and think of FOUR things that you can feel, and say them out loud. For example, you could say, I feel my feet warm in my socks, I feel the hair on the back of my neck, or I feel the chair I am sitting on.

3 - LISTEN: Listen for THREE sounds. It could be the sound of traffic outside, the sound of typing, or the sound of your stomach rumbling.

2 - SMELL: Say TWO things you can smell. It is okay to move to another spot and sniff something. If you can't smell anything at the moment or you can't move, then name your 2 favorite smells.

1 - TASTE: Say ONE thing you can taste. It may be the toothpaste from brushing your teeth, or a mint from after lunch. If you can't taste anything, then say your favorite thing to taste.

Take another deep belly breath to end.

You can always repeat the 5 4 3 2 1 exercise a few times - it may take a few times to get you in a calmer state of mind.

Also, you can modify this to a way that works for you. If you only want to focus on your first three senses (Look, Feel, Listen), you can do that instead.

# 9. Try Other Grounding Techniques

Maybe 5 4 3 2 1 Grounding isn't quite your speed. Here are some other ways you can get focused on the present moment that you may like more!

- Use the alphabet - say that alphabet slowly; say it backwards, say every other letter

- Use numbers - count to 100 by 7s, or count backwards from 50

- Remember the words to a favorite song

- Use water - splash water on your face, run water over your hands, take a tiny sip of cold water

- Carry a small object around in your pocket, like a stone or shell, or piece of fabric, and touch it when you need to be back in the present moment

- Notice and touch things around you - the desk, the couch, your pencil, your chair

- Make a fist and release it

- Think about all your favorite things or people

- Focus on a particular color - for example, name all the green things you see in the room

# 10. Take a Mini Mental Vacation

Your imagination is a powerful tool you can use to help you relax anywhere. Think about using your mind to take a mini vacation. Where do you want to go on your mini vacay?

- Do you love the beach, with the ocean waves, and the warm sand and sun?

- Do you love being in the woods, hearing the birds, and seeing the plants and trees all around you?

- Do you love a busy city, with buses and cars, and bright lights and lots of people moving everywhere?

- Do you love a quiet farm, with animals to care for and gardens to wander through?

Take a few minutes, and imagine a place that would relax you.

Use all of your senses to really go there.

If you love the farm, what does it sound like? What's the weather there? What types of animals are there and what sounds are they making? What are you doing while you're there? How do you feel? Go ahead and take a few minutes to take your own mini vacation, no matter where you are.

# 11. Use Visualization

Sometimes you are really worried about something that's going to happen in the future, like a presentation in front of your whole class that's making you super nervous. What you can do is visualize yourself doing that activity, and having it go smoothly, as a way to help prepare you and help you practice what it may feel like when you're going up there.

For instance, let's say you have a presentation in your biology class, and you're really nervous about it. Close your eyes, and imagine yourself walking into the classroom. What do you see on the walls? Is it warm or cool in the room? Now, imagine yourself walking to your seat and sitting down. Who is sitting around you?

When you sit down, take a few steadying breaths to help yourself get ready for the presentation. Next, imagine it's your turn to get up and speak. Imagine what it feels like to walk up the aisle, with your notes in your hand. Then visualize yourself facing your class, and while your heart may be beating fast, you feel calm and prepared. Imagine yourself taking a couple of deep breaths. Visualize yourself focusing on a couple of points in the room, maybe the back left and back right corner. As you speak, you look towards those parts of the room. You are speaking clearly, and you are delivering your presentation confidently. Then you finish, and you visualize yourself walking back to your seat and taking a couple more deep breaths. It's over!

As you practice and prepare your speech at home, you can visualize yourself going through the whole scene in your head to get yourself used to the idea of being in front of the class, and having it go well. This doesn't mean that it will go perfectly when you are in front of the class. It's ok to make a mistake -- everyone does! The goal of visualization is not to get you to give the perfect presentation, but to get you comfortable with an experience in which you may not have been comfortable before. This can work when you're going on a trip for the first time, or trying something new. You can visualize what it may be like. Even if it's not exactly what it will be like, that mental practice will help you feel more comfortable when you're in the real situation.

# 12. Create Your Own Mantra

Have you ever seen that video of the little girl giving herself a pep talk in the mirror? She's adorable, and while standing on her bathroom sink, she's reminding herself of all the people she loves and the things she thinks are great, and she repeats a phrase a couple of times, which I think is awesome.

*"I can do anything good!"*

You can find a word or phrase that resonates with you. Maybe it's from a movie, or a song, or just something you find helpful. You can say that word or phrase over and over again when you're facing challenges, or feeling overwhelmed. You can put that phrase on a sticky note and put it in your locker. Or write it on your mirror. Or have it on a stone that you can carry around with you to remind yourself of the word when you need it. Here are a few ideas for words or phrases that may help you:

- calm
- balance
- love
- strength
- resilient

- peace
- breathe
- grit
- You got this!
- You can do it.

# 13. Take a Drink of Water

Something as simple as taking a drink of water can help you calm down. If you take tiny sips of cold water, it can help you relax and calm down when you're feeling overwhelmed.

Dehydration, even mild dehydration, can have a negative impact on your mood. When you are dehydrated, your body can react in a similar way to how it reacts when you feel anxiety (headache, feeling faint, dizziness, feeling nauseated). Your body may think you're anxious, not dehydrated. Drinking water can help you stay more hydrated and may help improve your mood.

Plus, if you're at school, you can take an opportunity to give yourself a break and go to the fountain to take a little sip of water. Sometimes all you need is a quick walk and a sip to help you reset and get ready to focus back on the task at hand.

## 14. Use a Zen Garden

Zen gardens were first created in medieval Japan, and were added as part of a landscape to create a calming soothing space. They are supposed to reflect nature, and therefore include elements from nature, like stones, sand, and water. A zen garden space is purposefully designed to be simple, the goal being to inspire meditation and mindfulness. Sometimes you can find these zen gardens in fancy spas, or even in your neighbor's backyard.

When I worked in schools, I often had a zen garden that I would bring out for the students who enjoyed it. You can have your own mini zen garden in your room to help you de-stress and relax as well. All you need is a little wooden container, some sand, and a zen garden rake. You can add beads, stones, or shells.

Some people prefer to make patterns with the stones. Others prefer to rake the sand in a particular way. Other people like to smooth out the sand, make it even, and put beads in a row. Try playing with it and seeing how your body feels before and after.

## 15. Trace a Pattern

Tracing a pattern is a way of focusing on something right in front of you. It's a repetitive motion that can help calm your body down. The repetitive nature of tracing a pattern can be seen as a moving meditation practice. A research study found that children and teens with ADHD saw a positive behavior change when they were using a labyrinth or moving their hands through sand.

Patterns can be connected so that you can move your fingers in infinite directions, or you can have a line that you trace with your finger back and forth. You can use the patterns offered on the next page. Wherever you are, you can trace a shape on your desk, or on your hand. You could also use a sand tray or a patterned labyrinth. Try a few different patterns and see which one works best for you.

# Trace a Pattern

# PART THREE: WAYS TO USE MOVEMENT AND YOUR SENSES TO HELP CENTER YOURSELF

*"We see in order to move; we move in order to see."*

*- William Gibson*

People always talk about exercise as a main pillar of mental health. Why? First of all, the human body is amazing. It allows you to think, move, and interact with the world. It allows you to express yourself. How your body feels can have an impact on how you are emotionally feeling.

Exercise releases chemicals called **endorphins**. These "feel good chemicals" trigger positive feelings in your brain. So by releasing endorphins, you are tapping into a natural way to improve your state of mind. After a long run or an exercise class, your body might be tired but your endorphins are running high. You don't have to run a 5k to get it, either. Any type of movement will do this.

Your body also likes to have sensory input using your senses of touch, taste, smell, sight, and hearing. Maybe you like the way soft fabric feels, or maybe you love the sensation of holding a warm cup of tea. In this section, I focus on coping skills related to moving your body and using your senses to be centered.

# 1. Use a Weighted Blanket

Some people respond well to increased pressure on their body to calm themselves. Often, they use a weighted pad or weighted blankets. Studies have shown that using a weighted blanket can reduce anxiety, and help you get better rest. There are people who swear by their weighted blanket, and say it makes it easier for them to go to sleep and stay asleep. I've had several clients mention how much better they sleep when they use a weighted blanket. But keep in mind, it's not for everyone. Some people love them while others do not notice any difference or don't like the sensation.

If you are interested in trying one out, there are lots of stores online and in real life selling weighted blankets. You just have to make sure you are getting a properly weighted one. A weighted blanket should weigh no more than 5 to 10 percent of your body weight.

They are expensive, though, so it may be something you need to save up for or ask for as a present. If you are super crafty and good with a sewing machine, you can make your own using a fabric of your choosing and little beads. There are some great tutorials for making them on YouTube.

## 2. Take a Walk (In Nature, If You Can)

**I go to nature to be soothed and healed, and to have my senses put in order.**

**- John Burroughs**

Nature is a fantastic way to reset yourself. There have been numerous studies done about the power of taking a walk in nature to help you reset, and calm your body. Studies have also shown that being outside and around nature can reduce **cortisol**, a stress hormone. There are also studies that show nature can help people who suffer with depression by lifting their mood and providing motivation.

One study even showed that being in nature can increase our problem-solving skills and improve creative abilities. Some after-school programs and schools base their curriculum outside in nature because of the powerful effect it has been shown to have on mental well-being. It doesn't have to take a long time, even a 10-minute walk can be helpful.

You may not live in a place where you have easy access to the woods, beach or lake, and that's ok. There are also plenty of studies that talk about the benefits of taking a walk no matter where you are. A walk around the block in your neighborhood, at a local mall, or around your own home can be helpful and give your brain a break.

# 3. Use Cold to Cool Down

I once worked with a student who got angry all the time in school. He'd come in the door, and I'd immediately know he was mad - he was red in the face, his fists were clenched, and I could see the red rising on his neck. Sometimes, he'd even start to sweat. One of the first things I would do is give him a cold drink of water. If we were going to talk, I first needed him to cool off.

For clients experiencing that type of body reaction to anger, I always try to get them to cool down before we begin talking in earnest about what happened. When you are having a hard time, and your emotional brain is in charge, one thing that may help it reset is by using cold. There are several ways you can use cold to help cool your emotions down.

- Put a cold compress on the back on your neck
- Take a sip of cold water
- Chew on frozen grapes or berries
- Eat a popsicle
- Put a cold washcloth on your forehead or face

Hopefully after a few moments, you'll be in a calmer place and perhaps ready to chat with someone about what's going on.

# 4. Strike a Power Pose

Dr. Amy Cuddy is a social psychologist and has one of the most watched TED talks of all time about the power of your body language. Body language is a huge part of how we communicate with others, how others perceive us, and how we perceive ourselves. Dr. Cuddy talks about how you can change your emotions and feel more confident, simply by doing a power pose.

A power pose means putting your body in an open and expansive position that takes up space in the room. The most common example is the Wonder Woman stance, which you can do by placing your hands on your hips like a superhero, keeping your upper body lifted, and tilting your chin up. Another power pose is standing with your feet wide apart, and putting your arms up in the air in a V shape. You can do it for two minutes before you have to give a big presentation, or go in for a job interview, or before a big game.

You may want to give it a try before a presentation at school. I'm not saying you should do it in school in the hallway. Instead, do it at home in the morning before you get there. Or if you want to do it in school, go into the bathroom stall and try it out. It may also help if you use positive self-talk or say your positive mantra to yourself. I know it sounds a little silly, but if it helps you feel more confident, it's worth it!

# 5. Try Some Yoga/Stretching

There are so many benefits to yoga and stretching. It's become a popular offering even in some schools. Stretching and moving your body can help you practice deep breathing and being mindful. It's also helpful as a break in between homework subjects. Or you can use it as a way to wind down before you get into bed.

You don't have to do a 60-minute yoga flow to enjoy the benefits. You can just do a few simple moves, like the ones below, to get started.

If you are looking for more information for yoga/mindfulness, check out the **Resources** section for books about yoga and card decks.

*Before you start any exercise routine, please check with your doctor to get recommendations about what to do and what to avoid, based on your own body and medical needs.*

# 6. Drink Some Tea

Sometimes, what you need is a few quiet moments to soothe yourself with a cup of tea or hot cocoa. This can be an excellent sensory experience. You can also use this as a mindful moment. Focus on how the warm mug feels in your hand, how the steam feels on your face, and how great it tastes when you take a sip. This is the perfect opportunity for you to take a few moments to relax.

If you do this with a friend or someone you trust, this can be a great time to talk and share your thoughts and feelings in a safe place. If you struggle with Sunday night stress, maybe do this as part of your end-of-the-weekend routine. This can be a great thing to do as you get ready for bed.

To get more ideas for setting up your schedule and making a plan for self-care, check out the resources in **Appendix A: Wellness Worksheets.** There you'll find worksheets to help you really take a deep dive into your schedule and make plans for taking care of yourself.

# 7. Have a Snack

Did you know that snacks can make you feel more alert or calm you down? This has to do with the sensory input that I mentioned in the beginning of this chapter. You can use different textures and tastes to help alert or calm you.

To wake yourself up, you could try chewy foods like jerky, dried fruit, or cheese. Or you could try sour things like grapefruit, pickles, olives, or lemonade. Perhaps you prefer a little crunch, maybe pretzels, nuts, roasted chickpeas, or dried veggie chips would be more your style.

To calm yourself down, you can try smooth and creamy foods like yogurt, cottage cheese, applesauce, or guacamole. Warm foods like oatmeal or soup can also help, or perhaps sweet foods are more your taste - try grapes, berries or melons.

***As always, please be careful of food allergies. If you know you're allergic to something, or have had a bad reaction to it in the past, please don't eat it without consulting your doctor or allergist first.***

# 8. Pop Bubble Wrap

Bubble wrap is super helpful for carefully shipping delicate packages but it's also extremely satisfying to pop. When I get packages that use bubble wrap, sometimes I'll cut the wrap into small squares and keep it in a drawer. When I'm seeing a client who is having a hard day, or just needs to squeeze something, I pull one out and hand it to them. They get their feelings out, and often feel quite satisfied when all of the little bubbles have been popped.

Some people find it very relaxing and satisfying to take a square of bubble wrap and pop all the bubbles with their hand. Other people like to use their feet, and stomp on the bubbles to pop them. Just be careful if you choose to stomp on it, the plastic can be quite slippery. My recommendation would be to just use one foot, and hold onto a steady surface with your hands while you do it.

# 9. Create Your Own Sensory Space

Every person should have a room or space they can call their own and set up in a way that they find soothing and calming. When you think about your space, what can you do to make it your own? Can you make the lighting different, using a softer light bulb? Can you paint the room a calming color? Can you use soft blankets or cozy pillows in your bed? Can you make your room smell good by using something like a diffuser, or a room spray?

Even if you don't have your own room, see if you can set up a space that you can call your own. Maybe you share a room, but you can take a corner of it for yourself, and make it cozy and comfortable with your favorite stuff in it. Or maybe there's a space in a different room you could use. Even if you don't have your own space all the time, perhaps you could put your calm-space objects in a container and take them out to use when you're able to use them.

Of course, you will have to check with the adults in charge of the home to make sure your adjustments are acceptable. Please don't start painting walls before checking in!

# 10. Keep Your Hands Busy with a Fidget

A fidget is a small object you can hold, designed to help you concentrate at home or at school. I've had clients use fidgets when they are taking a big test or while they are doing schoolwork. Fidgeting keeps their hands busy, which helps them focus. I've also had clients use a fidget when they are giving a talk in front of the class. It gives them something small to hold onto and helps reduce their anxiety. I know younger students use fidgets frequently, and some of them may seem a bit babyish to you. Here are some items you can fidget with that don't look too juvenile:

- paper clips

- binder clips

- worry stones (small flat stones about the size of your thumb)

- pen caps

- bike chain fidgets

- ring fidgets

Please note: If a fidget distracts you from what you're supposed to be doing, then it's turned into a toy, and while it may be fun, it's not helpful for you when you're trying to get work done.

## 11. Use Mermaid Fabric

Mermaid fabric has gotten very popular over the last couple of years. It's a type of fabric made of colored sequins with one color on one side and a different color on the other. By sliding your hands over the sequins, you can switch the colors you see. You can make patterns in it, or just focus on moving all the sequins to the same side.

There is something satisfying and relaxing about moving the sequins back and forth. Some of my clients find it quite soothing. They also use it as something to fidget with during a session.As I've been out and about, I've seen mermaid fabric everywhere. I've seen it on pillows, clothing, stuffed animals, bags, journals, patches for your backpack, and even slippers. You can also put a patch on your backpack or on your keychain to have a coping strategy anywhere you go. A mermaid fabric pillow could be a great addition to your calm space at your home.

# 12. Use a Sound Machine or a Sound App

Soothing background sounds can be helpful as you are studying, doing work, or settling in to go to sleep at night. If you've been in therapy offices before, you may have seen/heard white noise machines. When they are used in offices, they're designed to give an extra layer of privacy. But there's another helpful side effect - they can be very soothing. In fact, I have had more than a few clients and colleagues tell me over the years that they CAN'T have the white noise machine on because it's what they use to fall asleep, and they'll get sleepy if we keep it on when we're meeting.

There are white noise machines that only make that whooshing sound, but there are others that can play other types of soothing background noises as well, like waves crashing or crickets chirping.

There are also apps available that can play a variety of sounds. I love the Relax Melodies app for creating your own unique blend of sounds. It has nature sounds, and city sounds, melodies, and audio scripts to help you relax. I also like the website/app Noisli. You can choose to focus on productivity or relaxation. The graphics are simple and the background on the website is calming. It changes colors over time, and is soothing. See **Appendix B** for more recommendations.

# 13. Move Different Parts of Your Body

Small body movements offer you the perfect brain break. You can do these as you sit in your class. No one even has to know that you're doing these things as a way to cope with what you may be feeling at that time. You can also do these in between different homework assignments, on the bus, in a car on a long ride, or just sitting on a couch or in your room.

Here are some ideas for how you can move different parts of your body:

- moving your head in a circle one way then the other

- rolling your shoulders back and then forward

- rotating your wrists by moving your hands

- rotating your ankles by moving your feet

- flexing and pointing your toes

- massaging one hand with the other

- tugging on your earlobes

- massaging the back of your neck and upper shoulders with your hands

# 14. Do a Little Exercise

As I mentioned at the beginning of this section, exercise is a natural way to release feel-good endorphins. A research team from Princeton found that physical activity can help protect your brain from stress and anxiety. Even small amounts of exercise can produce this increase in hormone production. You don't have to become a member of a gym and work out for an hour every day to do this.

Instead, try simple things like taking a walk around the block. Or you could do a quick workout in your home. You can take 10 minutes and do exercises just using your body weight, like squats, jumping jacks, push-ups, high knees, or sit ups.

You can make it a group thing by having a friend do something with you. You can go for a walk or take a barre class together. Or maybe you can even use it as a time to bond with your mom or dad or another trusted adult in your life. If they're into fitness, ask them about it or go along with them to the gym or for a walk/run.

***Before you start any exercise routine, please check with your doctor to get recommendations about what to do and what to avoid, based on your own body and medical needs.***

## 15. Take a Dance Break

## "Dance like nobody's watching."
## - Susanna Clark and Richard Leigh

Movement and music often go together. If you don't want to play or sing, or you just don't feel talented in those areas of your life, you can express yourself with your body. Moving to music can be freeing and fun, and can change your state of mind. Sometimes when you are in a bad mood, all you need is an impromptu dance party.

Dancing has helped me manage my stress and make new friends throughout my life. I've never taken an official dance class, but when I was growing up, I participated in show choir, and loved to dance with my sister and brother at home. When I was in college, my roommate and I connected through dancing. It helped us both get through an awkward and stressful time in our lives. Even now, if I'm having a particularly tough day, I like to go to a Zumba class to let it out.

You can dance in your own space by yourself if you want. Or you can find a group where you can do some dancing by taking a dance class, or an exercise class that is dance-based.

# PART FOUR: IDEAS TO HELP DISTRACT YOU

## "Even though you're growing up, you should never stop having fun."
## - Nina Dobrev

Why do you need distraction skills? First, it helps your brain. When you are in fight, flight, or freeze mode, your emotional brain is in charge. By doing something distracting, you're giving your brain a chance to switch back so that the thinking part of your brain can come back online.

There are other times it makes sense to use a distraction skill. There are going to be times in your life when you have gone over things in your mind. When you've processed things, you've identified all the things to explain how you are feeling, but you STILL can't get things off of your mind. You may find yourself perseverating on these issues, and unable to focus on anything else - at that point, it makes sense to use a distraction skill.

There also may be times when you're not ready to deal with everything just yet. You know you need to process things, but you're not at a place where you can do that fully. You can use a distraction skill until you are ready to face these issues.

However, I want to caution you. Please don't ignore your feelings. Don't stuff them down, because eventually they come out one way or another. And often when you suppress your emotions, they can explode without a lot of warning. I would recommend looking back at the first section, and trying one of those ideas to help you, even if it's just a few minutes, before you move into distractions.

So what are some ways you can help distract yourself? You can play! Play is a natural way for you to relieve stress. A time when you can relax and just do what you want is helpful for maintaining your mental health. Just because you are a teen doesn't mean you need to stop playing. Everyone, including adults, needs relaxation and downtime. The way you play may change, but you can still do fun stuff. You'll work much better when you allow yourself that time to do something fun.

Play is different for everyone. What one person finds enjoyable, another may hate. When my family and I went to Disney World, the ride my husband talked about wanting to go on from day one was Splash Mountain. He had fond memories of going on it as a kid. So, I agreed to try it out and give it a chance. Truth time: I hated that ride. My stomach still hurts when I think about it. However, my husband and daughter thought it was the BEST and wanted to go on it again. I said, "No thanks," and went over to "It's a Small World" (totally more my speed).

Figure out what you find enjoyable and relaxing, then take a few minutes to actually do it. In this section, there are 15 distraction skills you can use to relax during your downtime.

**"Play and unscheduled downtime are central to our emotional well-being throughout our lives."**

**- <u>Play = Learning</u>**

**edited by Dorothy G. Singer, Roberta Michnick Golinkoff, and Kathy Hirsh-Pasek**

# 1. Play an Instrument

Playing an instrument is another great way to use music as a way to cope. It can be exhilarating and cathartic to play. I've worked with some clients who are incredible musicians, and they express themselves when they play. They get out their anger, or express their worries, or show they are scared, all when they play. You can express so much emotion without using words while you play an instrument.

If you don't play a musical instrument, don't feel like you can't do this. There is one instrument we all have: it's your voice. We've all been singing in the shower or car and know how awesome that can feel. Sometimes the lyrics of a song speak to you and express what you're feeling about situations. You can also use your own words to express your feelings.

I watched a documentary about the experiences that kids face in the foster care system, and one boy in particular had experienced a mountain of challenges. One of the most powerful parts of the movie for me was when he was able to use his voice and share his thoughts and feelings on his story, in his own words, on his own terms, in front of a group of people he trusted and who cared about him. He used his voice to share his pain and hopes, and not only did it help him, and the others in the room as well.

## 2. Hang Out with a Good Friend

**"Friendship is born at that moment when one person says to another: 'What! You too? I thought I was the only one."**
**- C.S. Lewis**

Human beings are social creatures. When we share our thoughts and feelings with another person, it can expand our joy, and lessen our sorrow. When you find someone who gets you, who shares your sense of humor, or your interests, it's an amazing feeling.

When you hang out and have shared experiences, you are increasing your bond with one another, and creating memories together. According to a recent study, sharing the positive events in your life with someone who is supportive and listens to you increases the happiness we experience from those events.

We would all benefit from having someone in our lives who will not only enjoy who we are as people, but will also help us when we need to be pushed. We need that friend who will call us out in a kind way when we need it.

It's helpful to understand your own personality, because that impacts how social situations affect you. Some of us may be more introverted, meaning that you get your energy from being alone, whereas others are more extroverted, meaning you gather energy from being around people. Think about yourself for a moment, and which category makes the most sense for you. If you're not sure, think about these questions:

- Do I like working in groups? Or do I prefer to work alone?

- Do people say I am outgoing? Or do people say I am more reserved?

- Do I love having a huge group of friends? Or do I prefer just a few close friends?

Once you understand this about yourself, plan accordingly. If you are more introverted, make sure you take time for yourself. Just because you're introverted doesn't mean you won't enjoy a party, but you may be tired and need a little bit of alone time afterwards.

Just because you're extroverted doesn't mean you shouldn't spend time by yourself, but know that you also respond well when you have social time, so try to plan time to hang out with others on a regular basis.

# 3. Experience Something New

Trying something new can feel scary at first, because you're not sure what to expect, but it can also be thrilling when you've finished it. When you do something new, it has an impact on your brain - it lights up the pleasure centers of the brain and releases **dopamine**, another one of those feel-good chemicals. I'm not saying you have to go skydiving, but maybe just try a new food, or go to a new place you've never been before to experience some novelty.

Here's a fun bonus - when you do something new with someone else, it also helps strengthen your bond. You can try a new experience together with a friend, or with a family member.

Use the worksheet on the next page to figure out what new things you want to try. I gave you space to think about doing things alone vs. with someone, inside vs. outside, and things that are free vs. things that cost money. Take a few moments to dream and plan!

# New Things to Try

| Things to do alone | Things to do with others |
|---|---|
| | |

| Things to do inside | Things to do outside |
|---|---|
| | |

| Free Things to try | Things that cost $$ to try |
|---|---|
| | |

# 4. Help Others

When you are having a hard time, sometimes the best thing you can do is to help someone else. By focusing on someone else who needs support, you can take your mind off of what's bothering you and do something useful. Here are some ideas:

- Perform a random act of kindness

- Do a good deed for your neighbor

- Volunteer at a pet shelter

- Start a canned food drive

- Make blankets for kids who are in the hospital

Brainstorm and think about how you want to do something good for someone or some cause in your area. Then use your problem-solving steps to figure out how to make that idea a reality. Recruit friends, teachers, your school, or your family to get people to help you.

# 5. Hang Out with Your Pets

Pets have been shown to be a good source of comfort and support for their owners. They can reduce stress and increase **oxytocin** - a feel-good chemical - in your brain. Therapy dogs are becoming more popular these days - sometimes individual therapists or schools or mental health offices have them. I've also seen turtles and hamsters used as supports for children and teens.

When you have a bad day, you can take your dog for a walk or cuddle with your cat. You can play with your guinea pig or bunny, or make them new items to play with or decorate their habitat. Even having animals who aren't as cuddly can still be a source of comfort. You can read to a bird, talk to your fish, or hang out with your hamster.

Caring for pets is also a way you can focus on another creature's needs instead of your own, just like when you help other humans. It's a welcome (and sometimes cuddly) distraction.

# 6. Make Something With Your Hands

Keeping your hands busy can have a positive impact on your mental well-being. Knitters report that they use knitting as a way to relax and de-stress, and they say that it has a positive impact on their mood. Activities like quilting or crocheting are positive healthy coping strategies you can use.

These can keep your hands busy while you watch tv, help you pass the time, and give your eyes a much-needed break from a screen. Plus, you end up with a finished product when you're done. Even if it doesn't turn out perfectly the first time, you'll get better with practice. Who knows? You may discover a hidden talent you didn't know you had. And maybe you can even make things to give away to help others. Here are some ideas of things both I and my clients love:

- Knitting (on a circular loom or with knitting needles)

- Crocheting

- Sewing

- Quilting

- Rainbow Loom

- Weaving

- Collage making

- Woodworking

- Robotics

- Model Building

You may be thinking, that's a great idea, but how do I learn how to do these things?

First, see if there is anyone in your life who has one of these skills. My mom taught me to crochet, so I learned the basics from her. Or maybe there's an after-school club you can join, or a place where you can take lessons.

Second, you could get a book that teaches you how. I learned to knit from a Klutz book, and I learned all about quilting from books, too. I expanded my crocheting skills by learning how to read and follow patterns.

Finally, there are tons of tutorials on Pinterest and YouTube on how to do various arts and crafts activities.

# 7. Play a Board Game

I'm sure you've played games on your phone, but the games I'm talking about for this coping skill are physical games where you have to follow the directions to win the game. Playing card games and board games can be a great distraction. Many a snowstorm in my youth was spent playing a super long game of Monopoly. Playing games like Dungeons & Dragons are great ways to connect with others.

You could host a board game party at your home. Some areas now even have gaming cafes, where you can go and meet with other people who also want to play games. They either bring their own or use the gaming cafe's games, and make connections. You don't have to stick to Monopoly or Clue. There are tons of interesting games out there, here are a few you may want to check out:

- Exploding Kittens
- Apples to Apples Jr./Apples to Apples
- Settlers of Catan
- Escape Room in a Box
- Never Have I Ever Family Edition
- Bears vs. Babies
- Loaded Questions

# 8. Find Your People

Finding people who get you, who like what you like, who have the same inside jokes, is powerful. I used to work at a social skills clinic, where we ran all sorts of clubs - LEGO® Club, Pokemon Club, and Minecraft Society. The neat thing about this was seeing how the teens going to these groups started making friends.

By being in the same club, they automatically had something in common. It was easy for them to start conversations about the common interest they shared. For example, in the Minecraft Society, they would have animated discussions about the things they knew, tricks they learned, and things they loved about Minecraft. Then they would start getting comfortable enough to talk about other topics, and discover other things they had in common, which would lead to deeper conversations, and stronger bonds. In other words, **they would find their people.**

By identifying your interests, you can find people who could be potential friends. Maybe you love anime; you can join an anime discussion at your local library. If you love reading, maybe find a book club that reads the type of books you like. Once you find your people, you can then start to hang out more and do more things together outside of where you first met each other, maybe go to the movies or hang out at each other's homes.

# 9. Take a Screen Break

Listen, I get it. Being on a screen can be fun. There are so many things you can do on a screen - you can play games, watch videos, binge tv shows, and scroll through social media. But sometimes your brain needs a break.

It's not healthy to ALWAYS be on screens. Some studies have linked depression and anxiety to screen use. Are kids who are anxious and depressed using screens more? Or are screens causing anxiety and depression? I guess it depends on which studies you read. But the bottom line is, a screen break is a healthy choice, especially when it comes to social media.

Social media itself is tough, because what you see is not actually what real life looks like. Think about it. How many times do you post the first picture that you take? Do you just take the picture, or do you set it up, check out the lighting, make sure you don't look funny and your smile isn't weird. Those Instagrammers and YouTubers take time to put on makeup, get lighting right, clean the space behind them to make their house (and themselves) look awesome and perfect. It's totally staged. And that's ok, when everyone who views these images knows they are staged.

The problem comes in when we see these images and try to compare ourselves to the people in the photos. We can never measure up to that perfect life, or that beautiful face, because even the people in the pictures aren't happy and clean and perfect all the time. But that's how it can appear.

I have read several articles where people shared their Instagram or Facebook photos and then spoke about what was really going on when they took those pictures. One guy shared that he was out with a bunch of friends, and he took a picture that looked like he and his buddies were having a phenomenal time. He then shared that 15 minutes after he took that photo, he was sobbing because he was feeling depressed, and left the party without telling anyone.

> **"It's in our biology to trust what we see with our eyes. This makes living in a carefully edited, overproduced, and Photoshopped world very dangerous."**
>
> **- Brene Brown**

If you know that going onto social media causes you more heartache than happiness, then limit the amount of time you are on it. Don't spend hours scrolling through Instagram to see what others are doing, or checking out what's happening on Snapchat constantly. Also recognize that social media is not a true reflection of what's really happening. Yes, they may be posting awesome photos of how much fun they're having, but that's one moment of the time they are spending. They may be getting into arguments, or worrying, or maybe they were crying a few minutes before because someone is saying hurtful things. Social media very rarely reflects the whole picture.

Also remember that there are benefits to interacting in the real world. First, in order to sufficiently interact with someone, you need to be able to have a face-to-face conversation. Even with the rise of technology, you will still need to interact in real life. When you interview for a job, or attend college, or go on a date, you will have to interact in person at some point, so it's good to get practice doing it now.

## 10. Read a Magazine or a Book for Fun!

I know you read a LOT for school. Trust me, I get that. But remember when you used to read things for fun? You may not have a ton of time right now to read long books, but you could pick up a magazine or a graphic novel to read since they are shorter. Or you could re-read your favorite books from when you were a child. Rereading a favorite book series can be a great way to pass the time, make you feel nostalgic, and give you comfort.

During the summer time, when you (might) have a bit more downtime, you can read lengthier books for fun. Perhaps you'll even have the chance to pick the books you want to read for summer reading. When you pick books to read, choose ones that you find interesting; don't feel like you have to read Charles Dickens if you don't absolutely love classic literature. Instead, pick something that will engage you and bring you joy. You can also make a list of books you want to read. Ask friends for recommendations.

If it's challenging to read, or you don't have time to read, you can also listen to books on services like Audible. You could listen to books when you are hanging out in your room, and while you do something to occupy your time, like creating something with your hands, or coloring, or making something.

# 11. Make Plans for the Future

It can be hard to make plans for the future when it feels like it's so far away. But even if things are far in the future, you can start to make plans. You can plan for small things in the short term, like a trip to the new store that just opened, or a trip with a cousin to a new restaurant. Or you can also think bigger. What are the things you want to do in the next year? In the next two years? Five? Ten?

I had a client who had decided that once he lived on his own, he was going to get a pet chinchilla. He'd asked his parents, who refused to have a pet like that in their home. However, he was determined to get one once he lived on his own. Even though he was still living at home with his parents, he researched chinchilla habitats, their favorite foods, made lists of potential names, and made other plans for his future pet chinchilla.

You can go big picture if you'd like, and start thinking about where you want to live when you're out on your own. Do you want to stay where you are now, or do you want to experience a different part of your country, or the world? Are there places you want to visit?

Do you have ideas of what kind of job you want? Not necessarily the job you want

as an adult, but maybe a part-time first job. Do you want to work at Dunkin Donuts,

or are you more of a Paper Store type of person? Do you want to work at the busy

ice cream place during the summer months, or would you prefer to be a camp

counselor? Do you want to be a budding entrepreneur and start your own local dog

walking or lawn care business? Brainstorm and see what you come up with for

ideas!

# 12. Create a Positive Memories Box

When you are having a hard time, a good coping skill to use is thinking of the good things that have happened over the years. But it can be challenging to remember the good things in those tough moments. There is an easier way to call on those positive experiences and memories that you have - create a positive memories box.

You can fill this box with memorabilia from positive moments and life experiences. Maybe you had an awesome trip to the beach, so maybe you keep a shell to put in your box. Or maybe you found a penny by the basketball court. If you went on vacation, maybe you put in a souvenir you got while you were away. Maybe you keep the program from a play that you did where you made a new friend.

You can also keep a piece of paper or notebook, and jot down positive experiences that you've had. This is a great way to focus on the positives and what you are grateful for. It helps prolong the joy you feel when you've done something positive. Take a few moments to reflect and write about it, even if it's just a couple of words.

If you are really crafty, you can even make a scrapbook of positive memories. Do what works for you. To start right away, you can use the Positive Memories sheet on the next page to keep track of those awesome times!

# Positive Memories

# 13. Listen to a Podcast

Have you ever listened to a podcast? There are podcasts on every topic out there, like science, video game reviews, music, book reviews, history...practically any topic you want to find.

I've worked with several clients who are big Harry Potter fans, and there are lots of podcasts devoted to that book series. There's Harry Potter and the Sacred Text, the Real Weird Sisters, PotterCast, etc. There are also fiction podcasts. Sometimes they tell stories in parts, like Six Minutes or The Unexplained Disappearance of Mars Patel.

You can listen with a friend or a family member, which can lead to some interesting conversations. Even if you can't listen together, you can decide what you want to listen to and discuss it once you've both finished the episode.

Podcasts can also pass the time for long road trips. Find a new podcast and take a listen!

# 14. Watch a TV Show or a Movie

There are so many great shows and movies out there for people to consume. If you are having a hard time, you can easily lose yourself in a captivating show or movie. It can help you forget about what's going on for a bit, and give you a break. You could focus more on documentaries focused on real life stories, or you could watch something that is fiction.

Pick a show that seems intriguing and looks interesting. Maybe pick a show or movie that's based on a book you love. There is something enjoyable about reading a book, and then watching the movie the book is based on, and comparing the two. Or maybe you pick a show based on recommendations of friends who have similar interests to you. If they're into science fiction, and they recommend something like Doctor Who, maybe you give it a try too, and see what happens.

If something makes you uncomfortable, please don't feel like you have to continue to watch it. For instance, some people love horror movies. They enjoy the rush they get when they watch them, and they can go to bed with no ill effects. However, that is not everyone's experience when it comes to watching horror movies. View these instances as ways you can learn more about yourself, and be okay to say what makes you uncomfortable. Just because others do it and enjoy it doesn't mean you will too.

Another thing to keep in mind is that some tv shows and movies cover tough topics. If you are interested in watching shows with tough or sensitive topics, I would encourage you to watch them with a trusted adult or family member. This can make it easier to talk about any questions or concerns you have about the material you saw. If you happened to get distressed while watching, then it helps to have someone who knows you to be able to talk with you about it.

If you have watched something by yourself, and it was too overwhelming or troubling, and is still bothering you, please reach out and talk with someone. Don't try to handle it on your own. It is okay to talk about it.

# 15. Clean and Organize your Space

Sometimes when things feel out of control, it can feel good to find some control in your life. You may not have control of what's going on in your family, or at school, or with your teachers, but in general, you can control your space and your things. At home, you can clean your space, organize your books, sort your clothes, clean the bathroom, or clean the kitchen in your home. At school, you can clean up your locker to help you feel less disorganized and scattered, or you can offer to help out a teacher or secretary.

If you don't know where to begin, there are a ton of books out there about space organization and decluttering, like Marie Kondo's <u>Konmari Method</u>, or Gretchen Rubin's <u>Outer Order, Inner Calm</u>. For some people, having an organized space can help your brain get settled and focus better on the tasks you have.

If this doesn't work for you, that's okay too! Remember, not all coping skills will work for everyone!

# FINAL THOUGHTS

Whew! You made it all the way to the end! I hope you have found some new skills, and have tried some that have helped you feel better and manage your emotions in a healthy way. Overall, I hope you feel like you are better able to handle all the things life will throw at you.

I want to leave you with a few final thoughts.

**All feelings are ok**.

You can be furious, or sad, or worried. That's all okay. You are human and you're going to experience a range of emotions in your lifetime. What I want you to remember is that while all feelings are valid; it's what you do with those feelings that matters.

**Life isn't perfect, and that's ok.**

Listen, it's not going to be perfect. Life isn't perfect. Sometimes life sucks. Sometimes it's REALLY hard and horrible. But my wish for you is that you are better able to manage those moments when things go wrong in a way that's safe and healthy.

## Find one person you can talk to.

Talking to someone seems like a simple intervention, but it can do wonders for helping you. When you share positive things with someone else, your joy grows. When you share negative thoughts or worries with someone else, it lessens the pain.

Talking to someone can make it easier to process situations that are happening to you. You may see things differently, or be able to identify different thoughts and emotions you have around certain situations by chatting with someone. The other person can act as a sounding board, helping you figure out what went wrong, and what to do next. Having a conversation can also help you get ideas for dealing with your problems.

All it takes is one person you can trust. The key is to find one person in your life who you trust and feel like you can confide in. It may be your mom, or your uncle, or your older cousin. It may be your foster parent, or your music teacher. Or it may be your school counselor or individual therapist.

Find someone, and share what's really happening. Just make sure it's someone you trust, and someone whose opinions you respect. If you respect them, and think they are helpful and supportive, they are the best people to give you advice.

**Don't give up!**

Maybe using a coping skill won't work every time, but every time that it does work for you is a win, and a step in the right direction. Keep trying, explore different skills, and don't give up. I have faith in you, and I know you can do this.

# APPENDIX A: WELLNESS WORKSHEETS

Here are some other worksheets designed to support your work with practicing

coping skills, and help you focus on your own mental well-being and self care.

- Track What You've Tried

- Current Coping Strategies

- Weekly Schedule

- Self-Care Plan #1- Identify the clues that things aren't going well

- Self-Care Plan #2 - Make a Plan

**PROCESSING COPING SKILLS:** Check off when you've tried a coping skill. If you like it, check it off, then you can add it to your current coping strategies.

| Tried it | Liked it | Understanding and Processing Your Feelings |
|---|---|---|
|  |  | Identify Your Feelings |
|  |  | Recognize Feelings In Your Body |
|  |  | Be Prepared - Identifying Challenging Situations |
|  |  | Acknowledge What You Can and Can't Control |
|  |  | Identify Thinking Errors |
|  |  | Changing Your Inner Dialogue |
|  |  | Make a Plan to Solve a Problem |
|  |  | Think About the Best Thing That Could Happen |
|  |  | Express What You're Feeling in a Creative Way |
|  |  | Channel Big Emotions into Positive Action |
|  |  | Get Your Feelings Out on Paper |
|  |  | Write in a Journal |
|  |  | Write a Letter You Never Send |
|  |  | Use the Power of Music |
|  |  | Defeat Your Worry |

**RELAXATION COPING SKILLS:** Check off when you've tried a coping skill. If you like it, check it off, then you can add it to your current coping strategies.

| Tried it | Liked it | Relaxation and Mindfulness Coping Skills |
|---|---|---|
| | | Take a Deep Breath Using Your Hand |
| | | Take a Deep Breath Using Numbers |
| | | Use Technology to Take a Deep Breath |
| | | Be Mindful |
| | | Do a Progressive Muscle Relaxation |
| | | Do a Body Scan |
| | | Make a Gratitude List |
| | | Go Through 5 4 3 2 1 Grounding |
| | | Try Other Grounding Techniques |
| | | Take a Mini Mental Vacation |
| | | Use Visualization |
| | | Create Your Own Mantra |
| | | Take a Drink of Water |
| | | Use a Zen Garden |
| | | Trace a Pattern |

**MOVEMENT/SENSORY COPING SKILLS:** Check off when you've tried a coping skill.

If you like it, check it off, then you can add it to your current coping strategies.

| Tried it | Liked it | Ways to Use Movement and Your Senses to Center Yourself |
|---|---|---|
| | | Use a Weighted Blanket |
| | | Take a Walk (In Nature, If You Can) |
| | | Use Cold to Cool Down |
| | | Strike a Power Power |
| | | Try Some Yoga |
| | | Drink Some Tea |
| | | Have a Snack |
| | | Pop Bubble Wrap |
| | | Create Your Own Sensory Space |
| | | Keep Your Hands Busy with a Fidget |
| | | Use Mermaid Fabric |
| | | Use a Sound Machine or a Sound App |
| | | Move Different Parts of Your Body |
| | | Do a Little Exercise |
| | | Take a Dance Break |

**DISTRACTION COPING SKILLS:** Check off when you've tried a coping skill. If you like it, check it off, then you can add it to your current coping strategies.

| Tried it | Liked it | Ideas to Help Distract You |
|---|---|---|
| | | Play an Instrument |
| | | Hang Out with a Good Friend |
| | | Experience Something New |
| | | Help Others |
| | | Hang Out with Your Pets |
| | | Make Something with Your Hands |
| | | Play a Board Game |
| | | Find Your People |
| | | Take a Screen Break |
| | | Read a Magazine or a Book for Fun |
| | | Make Plans for the Future |
| | | Create a Positive Memories Box |
| | | Listen to a Podcast |
| | | Watch a TV Show or a Movie |
| | | Clean and Organize Your Space |

# Current Coping Strategies

| Relaxation | Processing |
|---|---|
|  |  |

| Movement/Sensory | Distraction |
|---|---|
|  |  |

# Weekly Schedule

It's important to know what your schedule looks like, and to make sure you have down time and time for fun activities. Use the weekly schedule below to fill in your schedule, thinking about everything you do - school, homework, sleeping, afterschool activities, jobs, etc. Feel free to make a color code with your activities so you can see how you are spending your time.

| TIME | SUNDAY | MONDAY | TUESDAY | WEDNESDAY | THURSDAY | FRIDAY | SATURDAY |
|------|--------|--------|---------|-----------|----------|--------|----------|
| 12:00 AM | | | | | | | |
| 1:00 AM | | | | | | | |
| 2:00 AM | | | | | | | |
| 3:00 AM | | | | | | | |
| 4:00 AM | | | | | | | |
| 5:00 AM | | | | | | | |
| 6:00 AM | | | | | | | |
| 7:00 AM | | | | | | | |
| 8:00 AM | | | | | | | |
| 9:00 AM | | | | | | | |
| 10:00 AM | | | | | | | |
| 11:00 AM | | | | | | | |
| 12:00 PM | | | | | | | |
| 1:00 PM | | | | | | | |
| 2:00 PM | | | | | | | |
| 3:00 PM | | | | | | | |
| 4:00 PM | | | | | | | |
| 5:00 PM | | | | | | | |
| 6:00 PM | | | | | | | |
| 7:00 PM | | | | | | | |
| 8:00 PM | | | | | | | |
| 9:00 PM | | | | | | | |
| 10:00 PM | | | | | | | |
| 11:00 PM | | | | | | | |

☐ School     ☐ Afterschool Activities

☐ Homework   ☐ Job

☐ Sleeping   ☐ Downtime

# Self-Care Plan

## 1. Identify The Clues That Things Aren't Going Well

Questions to ask yourself:

Have my eating patterns changed?

Have my sleeping patterns changed?

Am I exercising/doing some movment regularly?

Am I taking care of myself by showering, brushing my teeth,

washing my face, wearing clean clothes, etc?

**Below, write down the clues and signs that happen**

**when things aren't going well.**

# Self-Care Plan

## 2. Make a Plan

Questions to consider:

☐ What should my mornings and evenings look like to help me manage my thoughts and emotions?

- Ideas for the morning: stretching, doing a mindfulness activity, tracking your feelings
- Ideas for the evening: journaling, limiting screen time before bed, listening to a podcast or book

☐ Am I overscheduled? When am I going to do something fun?  (use the **Weekly Schedule PDF** to explore this)

☐ What coping skills will I use throughout the day? (use the **Current Coping Strategies PDF** list and pick 2 - 3 go to strategies for your day)

**Below, write down your plan to take care of yourself.**

# APPENDIX B: HELPFUL RESOURCES

## Crisis Resources

If you're in crisis, please tell an adult you trust.  It can be a parent, a grandparent, an aunt, uncle, cousin, or a good family friend. It can be a teacher, the school nurse, the school counselor. A member of your church, a coach, a dance teacher, etc. Even Lady Gaga encourages us to do this:

**"We gotta take care of each other. If you see somebody that's hurting, don't look away. And if you're hurting, even though it might be hard, try to find that bravery within yourself to dive deep and go tell somebody."**

**- Lady Gaga**

If you are in crisis, there are numbers you can call.

**<u>If You're in the U.S.:</u>**

24/7 National Suicide Prevention Lifeline at 1-800-273-8255

Girls and Boys Town 1-800-448-3000 (Text & Chat available too, visit http:// www.yourlifeyourvoice.org )

Crisis Text Line (U.S. only): Text HELLO to 741741

## If You're in Canada:

The new Canada Suicide Prevention Service (CSPS), by Crisis Services Canada, enables callers anywhere in Canada to access crisis support by phone, in French or English: toll-free 1-833-456-4566 Available 24/7

Crisis Text Line (Powered by Kids Help Phone) Canada Wide

free, 24/7 texting service is accessible immediately to youth anywhere in Canada by texting TALK to 686868 to reach an English speaking Crisis Responder and TEXTO to 686868 to reach a French-speaking Crisis Responder on any text/SMS enabled cell phone.

KidsHelpPhone Ages 20 Years and Under in Canada 1-800-668-6868 (Online or on the Phone)

## If You're in the UK:

24/7 Helpline: 116 123 (UK and ROI)

Samaritans.org: https://www.samaritans.org/how-we-can-help-you/contact-us

YourLifeCounts.org: https://yourlifecounts.org/find-help/

**If You're in Australia:**

Lifeline.org: https://www.lifeline.org.au/Get-Help/Online-Services/crisis-chat

LifeLine Australia: 1-300-13-11-14

YourLifeCounts.org: https://yourlifecounts.org/find-help/

Beyond Blue https://www.beyondblue.org.au/get-support/get-immediate-support

# How to Find a Therapist

There are probably already people in your life who may be able to give you recommendations for therapists.

Start with:

- Your pediatrician - Pediatricians may have a referral list of individual therapists who are experienced in working with teens.

- Your School Counselor/Guidance Counselor - Usually counselors in a school know of local resources that can be helpful, including local individual therapists.

- Your Insurance Company - this is a great place to start if you want to make sure that there aren't any insurance issues.

Other places to check:

- psychologytoday.com - you can search by zip code, specialty, or insurance. This is a great place to start looking, and reach out to people who seem like they might be a good fit.

- betterhelp.com - If you're 13 to 19, this is a place where you can see a therapist online. You can sign up for therapy with parental permission through this site, and you can message your therapist or schedule chat, phone, or video meetings with a therapist.

# Apps

## Apps for Breathing, Relaxation, Mindfulness and Meditation

**Relax Melodies** - https://www.relaxmelodies.com/

**Calm** - https://www.calm.com/

**Headspace** - https://www.calm.com/

**Stop, Breathe and Think: Meditations** - https://www.stopbreathethink.com/

**Insight Timer** - https://insighttimer.com/meditation-app

**Relax: Stress & Anxiety Relief** - https://www.saagara.com/apps/breathing/relax

**Breathing Zone** - http://www.breathing.zone/

## Apps to Track Moods

**Mood Meter App** - https://moodmeterapp.com/

**Daylio** - https://daylio.webflow.io/

**MoodKit** - https://www.thriveport.com/products/moodkit/

# Apps for White Noise & Soothing Sounds

**Relax Melodies** - https://www.relaxmelodies.com/

**Noisli** - noisli.com

**White Noise Ambiance Lite** - https://www.tmsoft.com/white-noise/

**Sleep Machine** - http://sleepsoftllc.com/

# Books & Resources for Yoga, Mindfulness, and Relaxation

## Books

The Mindful Teen: Powerful Skills to Help You Handle Stress One Moment at a Time (The Instant Help Solution Series) by Dzung X. Vo, MD, FAAP

Mindfulness for Teens in 10 Minutes a Day: Exercises to Feel Calm, Stay Focused & Be Your Best Self by LMFT Jennie Marie Battistin, MA

Mindfulness for Teen Anxiety: A Workbook for Overcoming Anxiety at Home, at School, and Everywhere Else by Christopher Willard, Psy.D.

Mindfulness for Teen Anger: A Workbook to Overcome Anger and Aggression Using MBSR and DBT Skills by Mark C. Purcell, M.Ed., Psy.D. & Jason R Murphy, MA

## Card Decks

**Yoga and Mindfulness Practices for Teens Card Deck** by Jennifer Cohen Harper Mayuri Gonzalez, and Argos Gonzalez, Illustrated by Karen Gilmour

**Be Mindful Card Deck for Teens** by Gina M. Biegel

**Self-Compassion & Mindfulness for Teens Card Deck: 54 Exercises and**

**Conversation Starters** by Lee-Anne Gray

## Audio/Video Mindfulness and Relaxation Scripts

**Dartmouth College - Relaxation Scripts**

https://students.dartmouth.edu/wellness-center/wellness-mindfulness/relaxation-downloads

**Relaxation Scripts from Inner Health Studio**

https://www.innerhealthstudio.com/

**Do You Yoga**

https://www.doyouyoga.com/10-cool-meditations-for-pre-teens-and-teens-67578/

**Coping Skills for Kids YouTube Channel**

Check out my YouTube channel for videos of Body Scans, Meditations, and

Progressive Muscle Relaxation scripts designed for teens.

# Books & Resources about Anxiety

Anxiety Sucks: A Teen Survival Guide by Natasha Daniels

My Anxious Mind: A Teen's Guide to Managing Anxiety and Panic by Michael A. Tompkins and Katherine A. Martinez

101 Ways to Conquer Teen Anxiety: Simple Tips, Techniques and Strategies for Overcoming Anxiety, Worry and Panic Attacks by Dr. Thomas McDonagh and Jon Patrick Hatcher

The Anxiety Survival Guide for Teens: CBT Skills to Overcome Fear, Worry, and Panic (The Instant Help Solutions Series) by Jennifer Shannon, LMFT and Doug Shannon

The Anxiety Workbook for Teens: Activities to Help You Deal with Anxiety and Worry by Lisa M. Schab LCSW

**Angst Movie** - angstmovie.com - a great movie that starts the dialogue about anxiety. Look for a screening near you on their website, or take action and work to set up a

**Anxiety Resources from Coping Skills for Kids** - copingskillsforkids.com/calming-anxiety   - My favorite resources & coping skills for calming anxiety all in one place.

# Books & Resources about Managing Anger

Anger Workbook for Teens: Activities to Help You Deal with Anger and Frustration

by Raychelle Cassada Lohmann, Ph.D., LPC

Chillax!: How Ernie Learns to Chill Out, Relax and Take Charge of His Anger by

Marcella Marino Craver

**Anger Resources from Coping Skills for Kids** - copingskillsforkids.com/managing-

anger

My favorite resources & coping skills for managing anger all in one place.

# Books & Resources about Handling Stress

Too Stressed to Think: A Teen Guide to Staying Sane When Life Makes You Crazy by Annie Fox M.Ed. & Ruth Kirschner

The Relaxation and Stress Reduction Workbook for Teens: CBT Skills to Help You Deal with Worry and Anxiety (Instant Help) by Michael A. Tompkins Ph.D., ABPP & Jonathan R. Barkin Psy.D.

The Stress Reduction Workbook for Teens: Mindfulness Skills to Help You Deal with Stress by Gina M. Biegel, M.A., LMFT

**Go Zen** https://gozen.com - programs for ages 5 - 15 focused on helping with anxiety, stress and worry.

# BIBLIOGRAPHY

Beetz, A., Uvnäs-Moberg, K., Julius, H., & Kotrschal, K. (2012). Psychosocial and psychophysiological effects of human-animal interactions: the possible role of oxytocin. *Frontiers in psychology*, *3*, 234. doi:10.3389/fpsyg.2012.00234

Berman, M. G., Kross, E., Krpan, K. M., Askren, M. K., Burson, A., Deldin, P. J., ... Jonides, J. (2012). Interacting with nature improves cognition and affect for individuals with depression. *Journal of affective disorders*, *140*(3), 300–305. doi:10.1016/j.jad.2012.03.012

Bloom, D. (2016, November 8). Instead of detention, these students get meditation. Retrieved from https://www.cnn.com/2016/11/04/health/meditation-in-schools-baltimore/index.html

Boston College (2019, May 22) *Understanding the Adolescent Brain* [Webinar Lecture]. Chestnut Hill, Massachusetts.

Burton, C. M., & King, L. A. (2004). The health benefits of writing about intensely positive experiences. Journal of Research in Personality, 38(2), 150–163. doi: 10.1016/s0092-6566(03)00058-8

Coldwell, W. (2019, May 13). Anger is an energy: how to turn fury into a force for good. Retrieved from https://www.theguardian.com/lifeandstyle/2019/may/13/anger-interviews

Cortina, M. A., & Fazel, M. (2015). The Art Room: An evaluation of a targeted school-based group intervention for students with emotional and behavioural difficulties. *The Arts in Psychotherapy*, *42*, 35–40. doi: 10.1016/j.aip.2014.12.003

Cuddy, A. (n.d.). *Your Body Language Shapes Who You Are.* Retrieved from https://www.ted.com/talks/amy_cuddy_your_body_language_shapes_who_you_are?language=en

Cuddy, A. J. C., Schultz, S. J., & Fosse, N. E. (2018). P-Curving a More Comprehensive Body of Research on Postural Feedback Reveals Clear Evidential Value for Power-Posing Effects: Reply to Simmons and Simonsohn (2017). *Psychological Science*, *29*(4), 656–666. https://doi.org/10.1177/0956797617746749

Dalai Lama Center for Peace and Education (2014, December 8). *Dan Siegel: Name it To Tame It*. Retrieved from https://www.youtube.com/watch?v=ZcDLzppD4Jc

Dean, N. (2019, September 5). The Importance of Novelty " Brain World. Retrieved from https://brainworldmagazine.com/the-importance-of-novelty/

dmchatster YouTube channel (2009). *Jessica's Daily Affirmations*. Retrieved from https://www.youtube.com/watch?v=qR3rK0kZFkg

Do Weighted Blankets Really Ease Sleeplessness? (n.d.). Retrieved from https://www.psychologytoday.com/us/blog/minding-the-body/201808/do-weighted-blankets-really-ease-sleeplessness

Ekman, P. (1992). Are there basic emotions? *Psychological Review, 99*(3), 550–553. https://doi.org/10.1037/0033-295X.99.3.550

Ekman, P. (1993). Facial expression and emotion. *American Psychologist, 48*(4), 384–392. https://doi.org/10.1037/0003-066X.48.4.384

Emmons, R., Emmons, R., University of California, & University of California. (n.d.). Why Gratitude Is Good. Retrieved from https://greatergood.berkeley.edu/article/item/why_gratitude_is_good/.

Emmons, R. A., & McCullough, M. E. (2003). Counting blessings versus burdens: An experimental investigation of gratitude and subjective well-being in daily life. *Journal of Personality and Social Psychology, 84*(2), 377–389. https://doi.org/10.1037/0022-3514.84.2.377

Evidence-based practice in psychology. (2006). *American Psychologist, 61*(4), 271–285. doi: 10.1037/0003-066x.61.4.271

Exercise reorganizes the brain to be more resilient to stress. (n.d.). Retrieved from https://www.princeton.edu/news/2013/07/03/exercise-reorganizes-brain-be-more-resilient-stress

Extraversion or Introversion. (n.d.). Retrieved from https://www.myersbriggs.org/my-mbti-personality-type/mbti-basics/extraversion-or-introversion.htm?bhcp=1

Froh, Jeffrey & Sefick, William & Emmons, Robert. (2008). Counting blessings in early adolescents: An experimental study of gratitude and subjective well-being. Journal of School Psychology. 46. 213-33. 10.1016/j.jsp.2007.03.005.

Ganio, M., Armstrong, L., Casa, D., McDermott, B., Lee, E., Yamamoto, L.,Marzano S, Lopez RM, Jimenez L, Le Bellego L, Chevillotte E, Lieberman HR. (2011). Mild dehydration impairs cognitive performance and mood of men. *British Journal of Nutrition, 106*(10), 1535-1543. doi:10.1017/S0007114511002005

Golinkoff, R. M., Hirsh-Pasek, K., & Singer, D. G. (2010). Play=learning: how play motivates and enhances childrens cognitive and social-emotional growth. Oxford: Oxford University Press.

Gray, Peter. Free to Learn: Why Unleashing the Instinct to Play Will Make Our Children Happier, More Self-Reliant, and Better Students for Life. Basic Books, 2015.

Harris , M. J. (2019, November 4). Foster. Retrieved from https://www.hbo.com/documentaries/foster

Hartling L, Newton AS, Liang Y, et al. Music to Reduce Pain and Distress in the Pediatric Emergency Department: A Randomized Clinical Trial. *JAMA Pediatr.* 2013;167(9):826–835. doi:10.1001/jamapediatrics.2013.200

Influencers Reveal the Truth Behind Perfect Instagram Posts - and It Feels Good. (2019, July 29). Retrieved from https://www.buzzworthy.com/truth-behind-perfect-instagram/

Kim, S., & Kim, J. (2007). Mood after Various Brief Exercise and Sport Modes: Aerobics, Hip-Hop Dancing, ICE Skating, and Body Conditioning. Perceptual and Motor Skills, 104(3_suppl), 1265–1270. https://doi.org/10.2466/pms.104.4.1265-1270

Lambert, N. M., Gwinn, A. M., Baumeister, R. F., Strachman, A., Washburn, I. J., Gable, S. L., & Fincham, F. D. (2013). A boost of positive affect: The perks of sharing positive experiences. Journal of Social and Personal Relationships, 30(1), 24–43. https://doi.org/10.1177/0265407512449400

Larkins, K. (2008, January 1). The Tranquil Zen Garden of Kyoto. Retrieved from https://www.smithsonianmag.com/travel/the-tranquil-zen-garden-of-kyoto-11696765/

Lesté, A., & Rust, J. (1984). Effects of Dance on Anxiety. Perceptual and Motor Skills, 58(3), 767–772. https://doi.org/10.2466/pms.1984.58.3.767

Li Q. (2010). Effect of forest bathing trips on human immune function. *Environmental health and preventive medicine*, *15*(1), 9–17. doi:10.1007/s12199-008-0068-3

McDermott, Jennifer F. Klau, Liliana Jimenez, Laurent Le Bellego, Emmanuel Chevillotte, Harris R. Lieberman, Mild Dehydration Affects Mood in Healthy Young Women, *The Journal of Nutrition*, Volume 142, Issue 2, February 2012, Pages 382–388, https://doi.org/10.3945/jn.111.142000

Moser, J.S., Dougherty, A., Mattson, W.I. *et al.* Third-person self-talk facilitates emotion regulation without engaging cognitive control: Converging evidence from ERP and fMRI. *Sci Rep* **7,** 4519 (2017) doi:10.1038/s41598-017-04047-3

Mullen, B., Champagne, T., Krishnamurty, S., Dickson, D., & Gao, R. X. (2008). Exploring the Safety and Therapeutic Effects of Deep Pressure Stimulation Using a Weighted Blanket. *Occupational Therapy in Mental Health*, *24*(1), 65–89. doi: 10.1300/j004v24n01_05

Nummenmaa L, Glerean E, Hari R, Hietanen JK. (2014 Jan 14) *Proceedings of the National Academy of Sciences of the United States of America.*;111(2):646-51. doi: 10.1073/pnas.1321664111.

Overview of National ADHD Research Study Utilizing a Double Finger Labyrinth Design. (n.d.). Retrieved from https://www.relax4life.com/adhd-research-with-intuipaths/

Physical Activity Reduces Stress. (n.d.). Retrieved from https://adaa.org/understanding-anxiety/related-illnesses/other-related-conditions/stress/physical-activity-reduces-st

Perry: Rhythm Regulates the Brain. (n.d.). Retrieved from https:attachmentdisorderhealing.com/developmental-trauma-3/

Plutchik, R. (2001). The Nature of Emotions: Human emotions have deep evolutionary roots, a fact that may explain their complexity and provide tools for clinical practice. *American Scientist, 89*(4), 344-350. Retrieved January 15, 2020, from www.jstor.org/stable/27857503

Researchers find time in wild boosts creativity, insight and problem solving. (n.d.). Retrieved from http://archive.news.ku.edu/2012/april/23/outdoors.shtml

Siegel, D. J. (2011). *Mindsight: the new science of personal transformation*. New York: Bantam Books.

Stillman, J. (2018, July 16). The More Miserable You Are, the Happier Your Social Media Posts, and This Twitter Thread Proves It. Retrieved from https://

www.inc.com/jessica-stillman/people-are-revealing-truth-behind-their-happy-looking-social-media-posts-its-heartbreaking.html

Stitchlinks - The Research Projects. (n.d.). Retrieved from http://www.stitchlinks.com/research1.html

Sutherland, J., Waldman, G., & Collins, C. (2010). Art Therapy Connection: Encouraging Troubled Youth to Stay in School and Succeed. *Art Therapy*, *27*(2), 69–74. doi: 10.1080/07421656.2010.10129720

Taren, A. A., Gianaros, P. J., Greco, C. M., Lindsay, E. K., Fairgrieve, A., Brown, K. W., ... Creswell, J. D. (2015). Mindfulness meditation training alters stress-related amygdala resting state functional connectivity: a randomized controlled trial. *Social cognitive and affective neuroscience*, *10*(12), 1758–1768. doi:10.1093/scan/nsv066

Wood, A. M., Froh, J. J., & Geraghty, A. W. A. (2010). Gratitude and well-being: A review and theoretical integration. *Clinical Psychology Review, 30*, 890 – 905.

Wood, A.M, Maltby, J., Gillett, R., Linley P.A., Joseph, S., (2008). The role of gratitude in the development of social support, stress, and depression: Two longitudinal studies. Journal of Research in Personality, 42 (4) 854-871, https://doi.org/10.1016/j.jrp.2007.11.003.

Zajenkowski, M., Jankowski, K. S., & Kołata, D. (2014). Lets dance – feel better! Mood changes following dancing in different situations. *European Journal of Sport Science*, *15*(7), 640–646. doi: 10.1080/17461391.2014.969324